# Praise for *The Future of Boards*

"As a Lead Director during times of corporate crisis, I have seen some extremely difficult governance challenges, namely, years of failing to resolve a company's important strategic issues, complicated by scandal in which the board lost trust in its CEO, along with dysfunctional working relationships between board members. *The Future of Boards* is most insightful and provides helpful wisdom and advice on virtually all of the board-related issues at the heart of these and other problems today."

—Robert Ryan, former Senior Vice President and Chief Financial Officer, Medtronic, Inc.

"As with all of Jay Lorsch's work, this is a thoughtful, perceptive, and insightful book. The contributors are terrific and the ideas highly informative and thought-provoking.

—Charles M. Elson, Director, John L. Weinberg Center for Corporate Governance, University of Delaware

"*The Future of Boards* is a blueprint for the future of American business corporations. It recognizes that the one-size-fits-all approach of corporate governance 'best practices' is not successful and cannot be the standard for the future. This book is a must-read for corporate executives, directors, government regulators and legislators, and all who are concerned with the way business corporations function."

—Martin Lipton, Founding Partner, Wachtell, Lipton, Rosen & Katz

"An insightful analysis of corporate boards and the key issues they are facing today. A great read for anyone interested in what corporate boards should be thinking about in the years ahead."

—William J. Mostyn III, Senior Vice President and Corporate Secretary, TIAA-CREF

# The FUTURE of BOARDS

# The
# FUTURE
## of
Meeting the Governance Challenges
of the Twenty-First Century
# BOARDS

## JAY W. LORSCH

HARVARD BUSINESS REVIEW PRESS
*Boston, Massachusetts*

Chapter Three, "Managing Your CEO's Succession: The Challenge Facing Your Board" in *Boardroom Realities*, Edited by Jay A. Conger, Copyright © 2009 by John Wiley & Sons, Inc. Reproduced with permission of John Wiley & Sons, Inc.

Chapter Four, "The Pay Problem: Time for a New Paradigm for Executive Compensation," Copyright © 2010 by Jay Lorsch and Rakesh Khurana. Reproduced with permission of Harvard Magazine, Inc.

Printed in the United States of America

10 9 8 7 6 5

Library of Congress Cataloging-in-Publication Data

Lorsch, Jay William.
    The future of boards : meeting the governance challenges of the twenty-first century / Jay W. Lorsch.
       p. cm.
    Includes index.
    ISBN 978-1-4221-8321-2 (alk. paper)
    1. Boards of directors.   2. Corporate governance.   3. Business ethics.   I. Title.
    HD2745.L67 2012
    658.4'22—dc23

                           2012002974

The paper used in this publication meets the requirements of the American National Standard for Permanence of Paper for Publications and Documents in Libraries and Archives Z39.48-1992.

# Contents

*Acknowledgments*     *vii*

Introduction     1
JAY W. LORSCH

ONE    Boardroom Challenges     7
*Lessons from the Financial Crisis and Beyond*
JAY W. LORSCH

TWO    Focusing on Strategy to Govern Effectively     37
KRISHNA PALEPU

THREE    Managing Your CEO's Succession     53
*The Challenge Facing Your Board*
JOSEPH L. BOWER

FOUR    The Pay Problem     77
*Time for a New Paradigm for Executive Compensation*
JAY W. LORSCH AND RAKESH KHURANA

FIVE    Board Governance Depends on Where You Sit     97
WILLIAM GEORGE

SIX    Recognizing Negative Boardroom
Group Dynamics     113
KATHARINA PICK AND KENNETH MERCHANT

SEVEN    The Argument for a Separate Chair     133
DAVID A. NADLER

EIGHT    The Argument for a Lead Director     155
RAYMOND GILMARTIN

*Index*     *175*
*About the Contributors*     *191*

# Acknowledgments

In addition to my colleagues who have contributed to this book, there are others to whom I should give thanks. First, I want to thank Srikant Datar, the Arthur Lowes Dickinson Professor of Accounting at Harvard Business School, who was director of the Division of Research when we began the project. He supported and encouraged us; without his presence, we might not have succeeded. I also wish to thank former HBS dean, Jay Light, and our current dean, Nitin Nohria, for their support. I want to thank my two research associates, Melissa Barton and Kathleen Durante, for their commitment to seeing this project through to its completion. They attended to the many details of data, exhibits, and even some of the writing that follows. Finally, I want to thank my assistant Jane Barrett, who, as always, has kept me and the manuscript in order.

# The FUTURE of BOARDS

# Introduction

In a recent conversation with the new CEO of a large U.S. global consumer-products company, I was surprised when she found it curious that I, as an alleged authority on boards of directors, was also a professor of human relations. Her comment caused me to reflect on how this came to be in an arena in which so much of the debate is about financial and legal matters. A possible explanation could be that I was derelict or lazy in not asking the powers that be at Harvard for a more appropriate title when I became interested in corporate boards twenty-five years ago. After a bit of reflection, however, I realized that what may seem a contradiction to some is really quite consistent with the way I and many of my colleagues in the Harvard Business School community, including the contributors to this book, see the issues of corporate governance and improving the effectiveness of corporate boards. Of course, boards are bound by legal and regulatory requirements, and they are deeply involved in financial and strategic choices. However, at the most basic level, they are groups of experienced part-timers from many different careers who come together to govern a company. Getting such groups to function as an effective governing body is, if nothing else, a challenge in establishing and sustaining effective human relationships, not only among board members, but also between the board and its top management, especially its CEO.

This fact is a central theme that unites the chapters of this volume. They cover major aspects of how boards must function to be effective governors of their companies in the future. Some focus on what boards should do—defining their basic role, overseeing strategic direction, and ensuring a flow of top-notch management talent. Other chapters focus on the choices about board leadership and the issues boardroom leaders face in successfully guiding their boards in these activities. But all the authors share the underlying belief that the most critical factor in boardroom success is the relationship among directors and how they engage with each other and their senior executives, especially their CEO.

What is particularly impressive to me about this shared belief is the fact that the authors have reached it through different paths. Two (George and Gilmartin) have been CEOs of major companies, and several (Bower, Lorsch, Merchant, Palepu, and Pick) are scholars who have studied boards as researchers. Most of us have also served on the boards of significant companies and, therefore, have the benefit of firsthand experience. Of course, what also unites us is our shared connection to the Harvard Business School. Whether alumni or current or former faculty, we have all been part of an institution that is committed to the idea that an important factor in all aspects of business success is understanding and dealing with the human side of the enterprise. This is as true in the boardroom as it is on the factory floor. The focus on the human element in the boardroom leads the contributors to discuss not only the interactions among board members and management but also the structures and processes that enable directors to work and interact effectively. As the title, *The Future of Boards*, suggests, I and the other contributors are also concerned with what lies ahead for boards. For one thing, we believe that there will be continuing efforts by some institutional investors to assert themselves and gain power vis-à-vis boards. Proposals from these shareholders may lead to new legislation or regulations for changes in the way boards function. In our view, such new requirements are quite likely to complicate the work of boards, but we also believe that the solution to this future problem rests in the ability of boards to navigate any such changes.

What is of more concern to us about the future is the likely growing complexity of the companies that boards must oversee. Globalization, the trend for increasingly rapid changes in technology in many industries, and the sheer growth in size of companies means they will be more complex. This fact confronts directors who in the past have had to overcome the constraints of time and a lack of deep knowledge of their companies with even greater problems in the future. In the chapters that follow, we provide our ideas for how boards can best deal with such challenges.

Although the reader can obviously peruse the chapters in any order, I have arranged them in the manner that makes the most logical sense to me. Chapter 1 reports on an interview study of forty-five seasoned directors of complex companies about their experiences leading up to the financial crisis of 2008. These directors point to the importance of being more proactive in defining their board's role, especially in strategic oversight as well as risk management and management succession. Doing all of this well means overcoming the limits of knowledge and time that directors of such companies face and performing the delicate dance of maintaining effective relationships with their company's top management.

In the second chapter, Krishna Palepu articulates his view of how boards can most effectively use their limited time to oversee company strategy. He outlines four basic questions about strategy, the answers to which every board must understand if it is to be effective in overseeing its company's strategy. With this understanding, the board can judge whether management is nurturing the key capabilities that attract customers and deliver value to them in a manner that leads to the desired financial results.

When asked what their most important job is, most directors will answer, "Selecting the next CEO." Although this decision is certainly one of the most important boards make, Professor Joseph Bower argues persuasively in chapter 3 that the responsibility for successfully developing the next generation of company leaders rests not with the board, but with its CEO. The board's role can only be to ensure that the CEO and other members of his or her top management team are doing the job of developing the next generation well. This means identifying potential future leaders, coaching them, and ensuring that they have assignments that develop their abilities. If boards do not encourage their CEOs to create such a developmental process, Bower argues, they may be faced with the alternative of finding a CEO from outside the company, an alternative that is more likely to lead to failed leadership.

In chapter 4, Rakesh Khurana and I offer a perspective on executive compensation that suggests that the persistent concerns about it are because the typical compensation plan is based on invalid assumptions. We suggest that directors, especially those serving on compensation committees, need to break away from these conventional thought patterns. Instead, they need to design compensation arrangements that truly motivate top managers to work together to achieve long-term company results.

William (Bill) George is one of the few people around who could have written chapter 5. Based on his experience as an independent director, a CEO, a chairman, and a chairman and CEO on ten different boards at different times, he describes how these experiences have shaped his views on the role of boards and the issues that board leaders and directors face in doing their jobs. From the perspective of an independent director, he discusses the challenges of becoming fully informed about the company and being able to make sound judgments about significant decisions. He also discusses an independent director's role in achieving a smooth CEO transition. His ideas on this topic provide an interesting contrast and complement to Joe Bower's ideas in chapter 3. Also from the same perspective, he addresses the problem of dealing with varying types of company crisis. He then describes his experience as a CEO working with a nonexecutive chair, as a CEO and chair, and finally as a separate chair himself. From these several perspectives he explores the issues of leadership in the boardroom. His experience in these various roles throws additional light on the discussion about the pros and cons of the various board leadership structures found in chapters 7 and 8.

Chapter 6, by Katharina Pick and Kenneth Merchant, focuses on an obvious fact with complicated ramifications. That boards of directors are groups of individuals working together is the obvious reality. The complicated ramification is that boards, like other human groups, are subject to a complex set of tensions that can and do lead to dysfunctional group dynamics. It is necessary for board leaders to understand these pathologies and to manage them as best they can to minimize their negative impact. Of all the chapters in this book, this is both the most novel and the most complicated to understand. However, the potential payout for the reader is a perspective on boardroom dynamics that can result in more positive decision making.

Chapter 7 ("The Argument for a Separate Chair," by David Nadler) and chapter 8 ("The Argument for a Lead Director," by Raymond Gilmartin) are in essence a debate about which leadership structure is best for boards and directors. I recommend that readers concerned with the critical question about what the best structure is for board leadership read both chapters. While each author states a clear and compelling argument for his position, they both understand the other's counterargument. By reading both chapters together, the reader will obtain a clear understanding of both leadership structures and their consequences. In the end, while each author argues for his preferred structure, they both recognize that each structure has strengths and weaknesses, and that boards need to use the model they prefer and ensure that it is working well. Each structure can and will work—what is not an option is not making a clear choice.

# One

# Boardroom Challenges

*Lessons from the Financial Crisis and Beyond*

JAY W. LORSCH

Numerous corporate scandals and failures have characterized the first decade of the twenty-first century: from the burst of the dot-com bubble in 2000 to malfeasance at Enron, Tyco, WorldCom, and elsewhere in 2002 to the demise of once-great automotive companies and the failures of banks and related financial institutions in 2008 and 2009. Each wave of business problems has been accompanied by accusations of failure on the part of corporate boards and by calls for government action. Indeed, passage of the Sarbanes-Oxley Act in 2002 was a direct result of the failures of WorldCom, Enron, and other mismanaged companies. Pressure from shareholder groups, the media, and politicians has prompted the U.S. Securities and Exchange Commission (SEC) to stiffen its requirements for reporting executive compensation in company 10-Ks. The financial crisis and recession of 2009 led to the passage of the Dodd-Frank bill, which, in addition to tightening regulations on banks, gave shareholders a voice in executive compensation ("say on pay").

This flurry of attention to boards of directors and corporate governance did not go unnoticed at Harvard Business School. Early in 2009, members of the faculty's Corporate Governance Initiative met to discuss the impact of the economic crisis on corporate governance in general and on corporate boards in particular.[1] We recognized the legitimacy of many issues raised by the media, the public, and politicians about boards' ineffective oversight of financial services firms and other complex companies whose failing contributed to the current recession.

As we reflected on how and why some boards had fallen short, we came to a tentative conclusion. The problems that surfaced in 2008 and 2009 largely differed, we believed, from those that had prevailed in 2002, when boards failed to identify and stop management malfeasance and fraud. By contrast, the more recent boardroom failures could be primarily attributable to the growing complexity of the companies that boards are charged with governing.

By *complex companies*, we mean those that operate multiple businesses (in terms of both products and geographies). In our view, these companies create unprecedented challenges for the executives who lead them and for the boards that oversee them. Such companies typically have at least two levels of general managers. The lower level are those responsible for individual products or geographic units, who make strategic, resource allocation, and human resource decisions within their purview. These general managers in turn report to the upper echelon of general managers, including the CEO. Ensuring an adequate and accurate flow of information from the lower level to the upper is a significant management challenge. Above this management structure sits the board of directors. Board members are largely dependent on management for an accurate and transparent flow of information. We questioned whether the boards of complex companies receive adequate information to understand the performance issues and risks their companies face. The challenge for the boards of such companies is how to oversee such complexity within the limited time that directors can devote to the task.

We agreed that the best way to test these conclusions and explore the causes of board failures was to go directly to the source: directors serving on the boards of financial institutions and other complex companies. We decided to seek answers to two broad questions: How well did these boards function before the recession, and, more important, what aspects of board functioning troubled board members as they looked to the postrecession future?

Our approach may seem unorthodox to other academics, but we concluded that it would provide the most accurate and thorough answers possible to our two questions. Eight senior members of our faculty, all of whom serve on boards themselves, agreed to interview five directors each. We selected as interviewees (1) members of boards of complex public companies whom we both (2) knew personally and (3) believed to be both dedicated and respected by fellow board members. Clearly, this was not a random sample. It was intended to be biased toward experienced directors with whom we had prior relationships and therefore had reason to believe would be candid with us.

We interviewed forty-five directors. Table 1-1 characterizes the companies they represented (while preserving the anonymity of both director and company, a condition we established to encourage candor). We believe that the interviewees were frank both about their boards' strengths and about specific needs for improvement.

Interviewees' opinions varied about the difficulties that complexity poses for boards, but there was strong consensus that the key to improving boards' performance is not government action but action on the part of each board. Several directors worried that the government would take action if boards themselves did not.[2] One director articulated the challenge: "How should the board help the company avoid embarrassment and reputational damage, and not allow the government to run the companies because we don't step up and do what we're supposed to do?" More state or federal regulations and rules were seen as unneeded

TABLE 1-1

**Interviewees' companies by industry and size in 2008**

| Industry | Number of companies | Average market capitalization, 2008 (in millions of $) | Average sales, 2008 (in millions of $) |
|---|---|---|---|
| Consulting | 2 | 12,745 | 18,722 |
| Consumer discretionary | 18 | 28,485 | 47,618 |
| Energy | 2 | 34,064 | 34,164 |
| Financials | 14 | 16,601 | 24,535 |
| Health care | 11 | 30,797 | 19,475 |
| Industrials | 8 | 32,639 | 42,661 |
| Information technology | 16 | 23,812 | 18,713 |
| Materials | 4 | 6,776 | 18,816 |
| Telecommunications | 2 | 106,051 | 107,323 |
| Utilities | 1 | 15,739 | 13,094 |
| **Total** | **78** | **26,210** | **31,346** |

and apt to produce unintended consequences that could damage boardroom effectiveness. In the view of these directors, each board must develop structures, processes, and practices that fit the needs of the company and its business(es); the notion that "one size fits all" was viewed with extreme skepticism. In essence, there was a strong consensus that the key to successful governance rests in the hands of each board. Specifically, it resides in how directors work together and with management to oversee the company and make decisions. In the directors' view, these are matters that cannot be regulated effectively by government.

The directors also expressed the view that organizations representing shareholders, such as RiskMetrics and Glass Lewis, have become too formulaic and prescriptive. This phenomenon has led to a check-the-box mentality whose efficacy several directors questioned. "I think there's a lot of focus put on meeting metrics set by outside parties today. I'm not entirely certain that's a good thing, but certainly . . . so-called proxy governance firms, like RiskMetrics and so forth, have become the de facto regulators as it relates to corporate governance," one director said. "And increasingly these guidelines shift annually, requiring boards to monitor changes that are going on, and to adjust. So it's kind of become a bit of a shifting-sand environment in that regard." Another director concurred: "I saw . . . a certain attitude which was form over substance. In many board meetings, I realized, just 'Let's address the formal issues—tick, tick, tick the box—and now let's get to business.' I think people should be aware that form is not substance, and form should not be overdone; otherwise it goes to box-ticking."

The directors agreed that they should function as long-term stewards of their companies. Given this perspective, it is not surprising that they also worried about the short-term focus on shareholder value that has come to dominate the U.S. economy. Specifically, they were critical of the agency theory promulgated by former Harvard Business School professor Michael Jensen. According to this theory, directors must act as agents for their companies' shareholders. While recognizing their fiduciary duty to the shareholders who technically elect them, our respondents were typically acutely aware that they also have a legal responsibility for the long-term health of the company. Furthermore, they recognize that shareholders are often short-term investors with no long-term commitment to the company. In sum, these directors tended to be uncomfortable with the notion that they can or should act only as shareholders' agents. As one senior executive put it, "We are transitory managers of a permanent institution."

This chapter will first briefly explain how the interviewees characterized the strengths of their boards. Then it will examine in more depth six areas in which they identified shortcomings or need for improvement:

- Clarifying the board's role

- Acquiring better information and deeper knowledge of the company

- Maintaining a sound relationship with management

- Providing oversight of company strategy

- Ensuring management development and succession

- Improving risk management

Finally, the chapter will discuss two issues that appeared not to trouble our informants but that our own experience leads us to view as significant: executive compensation and the relationship between the board and shareholders.

## Prerecession Boards

The directors generally reported that their boards had grown more effective in recent years and that the quality of their fellow directors had improved. For one thing, the number of independent directors had increased. "There was a movement toward all independent directors, with the exception of the CEO," one director reported. These new directors also seemed better qualified than their predecessors. "I think the boards that I am on have all recruited new members," another director told us, "and I would say have significantly upgraded the board—fewer of the cronies and the old-timers, and more of the real professionals, experienced people who have some 'value add' to the board." Another commented, "I'm impressed by the quality of the people that are willing to provide time. They're frequently a mix of people who have expertise in a particular area that is important to the company, people who have operations or CEO experience, or people who have financial or Street experience. They typically are very impressive. I think it is important to make sure that there is some breadth of experience, because it does provide you with insights that are hard to get otherwise."

Some directors who remained uneasy about the sufficiency of relevant experience on boards questioned the regulatory emphasis on independence. "I don't think independence is anywhere near as important as people thought it was," one such director commented.

"I think it was a red herring." Independence—a focus of recent regulatory changes—is a subject to which we shall return, related as it is to the question of how well directors understand their company.

Another positive sign is the growing comfort of boards' audit committees and other directors about meeting the requirements of the Sarbanes-Oxley Act. "I think by 2007 we kind of felt that the pendulum was swinging back," one director commented. "We felt comfortable about the company we were involved in, that there wasn't any monkey business, there weren't any back-dated options, there were none of the various types of scandals that we tested for in all of these companies. And so I think we felt good about that, and so therefore could begin by 2007 to think again about strategy, big picture. Where are we really going, and where are the opportunities?"

## Issues Highlighted by the Recession

Though most of the directors believed that their boards had been on a positive trajectory, the credit crisis and subsequent recession raised deeper and more basic issues for many. Most frequently mentioned were two linked questions: What role is appropriate for the board? And how can the directors understand enough about the company to meet their responsibilities effectively? We shall discuss each question in turn.

### The Board's Role

Why so many directors were reflecting on the board's role is difficult to pinpoint. A partial answer undoubtedly rests in the fact that regulations and laws offer little guidance about what boards are supposed to do. In most states the basic statute that describes the purpose of boards is phrased very broadly. For instance, in Delaware, which sets the standard for other states, directors find little help in the statute that defines their job: "The business and affairs of every corporation shall be managed by or under the direction of a board of directors."[3] This statute also tells directors that they may delegate the actual running of the company to its officers. Court decisions related to director conduct are largely focused on matters of process—that is, on *how* boards are to carry out their duties. For example, directors must exercise good business judgment and be loyal to the corporation. As one director told us, "Our board lawyers say, 'You know, the board members are not supposed to be making the management decisions. You're just supposed to be comfortable that the management is going through the appropriate processes to come to well-thought-out decisions.'"

Given the prevailing lack of specificity about their duty, most boards gradually develop an implicit understanding of what their job should be. As long as the business was thriving and management was comfortable with what the board was and wasn't doing, there was no need for greater explicitness. But the economic shock of 2008 appears to have caused many directors to reconsider what their boards had been doing and to question whether they could or should be acting differently. "I really do think it's time for a lot of reflection by boards right now about what we could have done better in the last six months to a year," one director said. "What did we miss? I think it's always great to have time to reflect backward about what we learned about what we've just been through, or what we're going through, and how we could have served the shareholders better if we had spent our time a different way."

Directors' reflections on the board's role had multiple dimensions. For some, the question was whether and how exclusively the board should focus on compliance with applicable laws and regulations. In their view, the board's primary role is to be rules-oriented. Others viewed compliance as the job of lawyers and conceived of the board's job much more broadly. "I'm more comfortable on some boards than I am on others," one director told us. "Some people have really taken the value of governance, the importance of governance, to heart, and it pervades the company. Others have been slower to that realization, and tend to view governance as something that the lawyers are driving. And therefore it is something that, at the attitude level, slows things down; it's a cost to the enterprise. It gets in the way of being efficient about decision making and moving forward."

This director and a handful of others seemed to be struggling with a hangover from the effects of Sarbanes-Oxley and other regulations, which absorbed so much board time a few years ago. To others, the financial crisis itself meant that boards should intensify their efforts at compliance: "In adversity, boards become more active by definition," one director said. "But what one has to ask is: Should they be more active when things are good, to make sure that the risk-management processes are in place, that the financial-control processes are in place, so that they're assured that the organization has the controls and procedures that will red-light or highlight risks when they need to be highlighted?"

Other directors disagreed, believing that the board should devote less time to compliance issues and more to substantive business matters. Doing both is not easy, as one director pointed out: "Just the challenge of fitting all of the compliance activities that boards and their committees have to execute on, while still doing these broader and perhaps more interesting things that boards are supposed to do—in terms of providing oversight of the business, oversight of management, particularly oversight of the CEO, as well as engaging in the strategy and the direction of the company—is difficult." For directors like this one, the central issue was how much directors could be expected to do. "I think that the expectation of what a board can or cannot do, either in the public perception or even in the regulatory perception, is overstated," another director said. "At times this is a big challenge for board members. They feel they should be doing more, but doing more is difficult to do." Such comments suggest that, in times of crisis, directors feel a responsibility to take a larger role but aren't certain how to do so.

One director pointed out a significant problem that arises when boards contemplate becoming more engaged: "I think the board is more involved. I think it's busier. I think boards have to be more focused. And I think they have to be careful that they don't start trying to manage the company. They have to give the guidance, or set the trends, but they can't be managing the company." Where to draw the line between the board and management troubled our interviewees. Two directors' comments effectively capture the two sides of the debate. One said, "In today's environment, where there is so much pressure on directors, I think there can be a tendency for directors to want to cross the line a little too much sometimes, on the operating side, probing committees on every little subject that comes up." In sharp contrast, another director said, "At the moment, boards are reluctant to be intrusive into the day-to-day operations. And I think they are reluctant to be intrusive on the personnel management, beyond the top guy and maybe the heir apparent, if there's a change coming. And so they isolate themselves from understanding where the risks are coming from and what those risks are. I don't think they can do the job without becoming more involved."

Whereas these directors puzzle over where the line should be drawn between management and the board, others believe that the crucial issue is how the board interacts with management regarding major decisions. "I've always thought the board should be a catalyst," one director said. "They need to make sure that there's really good open dialogue, and all the dimensions and possibilities are at least given some air time. I think the board's role is to make sure that management, if they are not having these discussions with the board, does have these discussions with the board. And if they're not working on it, they should be working on it." Another director asserted that the board should be even more proactive: "I think the board has to lead more. And the shareholders may not even like that too much, and the management may not like it. But I think the board has to say, 'Wait a minute, what steps are we taking while we're still making that profit on one product? What are we going to do so that we're ready in five years with another new product?'"

As we shall see, directors' preoccupation with better defining the board's role is also linked to their views on board involvement in shaping company strategy. Both questions turn on another matter: how well the board understands the company.

*The Board's Understanding of the Company*

The thoroughness of the board's understanding of the company was second only to the issue of the board's role in frequency of references during our interviews. We use the term *understanding* because it expresses what the directors seemed to be seeking. They often used the words *knowledge* and *information* as well, but their underlying concerns were clearly insufficient understanding on the part of some boards, the causes of this phenomenon, and what they and other directors could do about it. This issue should be examined in the context of growing corporate complexity, since the companies in question are typical of the complex corporations alluded to earlier. Such companies are particularly difficult for their directors to understand.

One director spoke about what can transpire when a company is complex and about the possible corrective effect of an expectation that the board should understand the company's transactions: "I think a head of a company looking at the sustainability and the long-term future of the company should never allow somebody in the company to get in any deal which is not fully understood by the board and by the shareholders. And the best check is that the CEO should be able to speak about all deals which are made." The same director emphasized the need for directors to fully comprehend the company's business model: "My experience is that it's of utmost importance that the board has a full understanding of the business model . . . entry barriers, competitors, technological changes and so on. A full understanding of the business model—which includes, of course, what are competitors doing, what are the trends in the market, and so on."

As important as they believed it to be to understand the company, some directors admitted that complete understanding is an impossibility: "You really can't understand everything that's going on in the company, and the notion that you can is misguided," one director said. "Unfortunately, I think people do expect directors to know a lot more than they sometimes do."

A disproportionate number of those who attested to the elusiveness of adequate understanding were directors of financial-service firms. "We had the Enron era; now we have the financial era, where we're taking down the whole world with us, and it can't be because all these people are stupid," one such director said. "It has more to do with the depth of understanding of what's really going on." Another was even more pointed: "[Two banks]—I think they crashed and burned. Neither one of them had anybody that I could detect on the board that's had any serious financial skills. And it doesn't look to me like those boards demanded to know what was happening off balance sheet." A third director concurred but questioned top management's financial skills as well: "The bank boards and the bank CEOs and leadership, obviously, with the exception of maybe one or two, did not understand the risks that they were managing. Clearly, the bank boards were in over their heads, just like the CEOs were. They didn't understand the paper they were issuing and how the risk was being syndicated, all that."

Finally, one director pointed out that even when a board meets as often as ten times a year (the typical U.S. board meets six times), it is impossible for directors to understand complex financial companies: "One has to understand that, at the beginning of this, that board members show up, at a maximum, let's say fifteen to twenty days a year. Maximum. And the idea that board members would be close enough, informed enough, experienced enough, engaged enough to have seen some of this coming, and even more, to have been wise enough to figure out how to duck, is just naïve in the extreme."

Such comments raise an obvious question: Why do directors have such difficulty understanding their companies? Several directors commented on the scarcity of specific industry knowledge on most boards. "I think our thinking is going to be forced to be changed by virtue of the financial crisis, in that I think we're going to place higher value on industry-specific knowledge and less on general knowledge of governance and the general experiential things that come with an all-purpose board," one director said. Another echoed this view: "The board needs to be asking the right questions. One thing that I've seen just over the last couple of years, and been a champion of, is having at least one board member who is very knowledgeable about the business you're in . . . It really is helpful, particularly in executive sessions, when you don't have the management there, and you're debating something, or wondering whether you should be worrying about something, to have someone who understands the business a little bit better than you do."

A third director went further, linking the shortage of specific company knowledge to corporate-governance reforms that called for more independent directors: "Strategy is harder, because it requires a familiarity with the business, and an understanding of it, in order to make any sort of informed suggestion. And clearly, I think, if you were to look at boards, there are still huge deficits in certain technical expertise and understanding of the business that persists at boards . . . One of the things that's been lost, in this notion of full independence and limited insiders and split chairmen and CEOs, is that boards have lost insight into the business as a result of not having, if you will, as free and consistent access to people who are steeped in the business as they might otherwise have."

This final point deserves emphasis. We believe that a major reason directors find it difficult to understand their companies is that the typical board of a large public U.S. company consists entirely of directors who must meet the test of independence. As a practical matter, it is difficult, if not impossible, to find directors who possess deep knowledge of a company's process, products, and industries but who can also be considered independent.

A second reason that directors have difficulty understanding their companies' business is that they are heavily dependent on management, especially the CEO, to know what is going on. One director explained the frustrations of such dependence: "Whether [an automobile manufacturer] should close their European operation, [management has] much more insight and information than the board has, and they have gone through a thorough evaluation. They make a recommendation, and you're more likely to agree with it than not, even after you have questioned them very closely, because you do not have nearly the amount of information they have. It's not that they're withholding the facts from you, but you're just not as close to it. I find that very frustrating." A second director agreed: "I think where the board gets caught, interestingly enough—and the board will probably figure out how to fix this—but it got caught relying far too much on the top guy to tell them what's going on."

A third director itemized specific aspects of the challenge that directors face in judging the validity and veracity of what management tells them; he also described the changes his board had implemented in response to a recent crisis: "It was significant in terms of information that we requested and management began to bring forward: the kind of information, the way it was brought forth, the form in which it was presented and the amount of time spent on some kinds of reports rather than others. We didn't change the board structure or the committee structure. But we changed the info flow and the feedback and the transparency, one might say, between the board and management on certain issues."

Directors do not merely have difficulty assessing the answers they get from management; they also have trouble knowing which questions to ask. "A board only knows what it's told. You can ask a question and be given an answer—but maybe it's not the right question, or maybe the answer is true but doesn't exactly get you where you need to go," one director explained. "But more fundamentally, management basically provides the material at a board meeting, and if you don't live day to day in the company, you're not going to know whether in fact you are hearing all the relevant aspects of it, the good, the bad, and the ugly. You're not going to know. And I've got to tell you, I've lived through too many of those."

So what can directors do to achieve greater understanding and deeper insights? Our directors discussed two approaches. The first was, as they put it, to "dig deeper" in discussions with management. "We always run with this concern that we don't want to manage the company. But we want to direct the company . . . Asking detailed questions to understand more fully what's going on in a company is, I think, a requirement to be an effective director, not managing," one director told us. He added: "I have no insight about what we should do until I have significant insight as to what's really going on, and you can't get that by somebody doing a PowerPoint presentation."

Such comments imply that, to be effective, directors must be willing to keep pushing and questioning until they are confident that they thoroughly understand the issues involved in any decision or assessment they make. As we shall see, a complication of this approach is that it is off-putting to management to be pressed for answers. As we shall also see, directors want to maintain a cordial relationship with management.

A second approach—the two are not mutually exclusive—is to seek sources of information and knowledge beyond the management team. As one director put it, "Boards need to somehow find broader sources of information, so they're not relying on one or two people." Another suggested that directors need to seek out company stakeholders other than management to talk to: "Whether it's once in a while meeting with shareholders, once in a while meeting with the representatives of the employees, whatever, I think it's really important, particularly in difficult times like we are in, and are going to be in for some time, for the board to see actual underpinnings of the company."

A third director advocated seeking broader sources of information but acknowledged that such approaches eat up time: "There is no substitute for time spent meeting with management of the different divisions or sectors that are the next level down the corporate ladder, having them present directly to the board, visiting operations, . . . getting in the field, getting a sense of operations— not interfering, but understanding on a more hands-on level."

As this comment indicates, digging more deeply takes time, and directors already face constraints on the time they can make available, both for preparation and for meetings. The directors we interviewed seemed willing to invest the time needed, but at some point even they will encounter limits on the time they can devote to gaining greater understanding. Furthermore, as our informants noted, it is important to be sensitive to management's feelings and to find ways to seek more profound understanding of the company without putting more strain on the board's relationship with management.

## The Relationship Between the Board and Management

When directors spoke of management, they were often implicitly referring to the CEO. Meanwhile, however, they were aware that the board's relationship with the CEO is affected by its relationships with other senior executives.

According to our informants, the board's relationship with management has several dimensions. Perhaps the most obvious, in their eyes, is the division of decision-making responsibility between the board and management—what both parties call "the line between the board and management." This line is not drawn in concrete; it is more like a line drawn on a sandy beach, according to these directors, because it can be erased and redrawn elsewhere in response to circumstances.

One factor that affects the positioning of the line is the nature of the business challenges that the company faces. As one director told us, "[At one company that] has gone through some recent challenges, I would say the board started at a high level, and, with the challenges the company has had, it descended into deeper and deeper, longer meetings, and deeper involvement in the business. And in that case management is trying to figure out quite how this works. So the board and management are sort of working with each other, with respect and a high level of collegiality, but are also a little wary of each other as we try to redefine what the role is and how deep we get and how deep we don't get." Another director was more succinct: "Even when a company is in trouble, the board gets more involved but still is limited in what it can accomplish other than replacing the CEO."

A second factor that influences where directors draw the line is their degree of confidence in the CEO. "Where the CEO hasn't changed recently, my sense is—and my own experience is—that committee activity, board activity, and board leadership, as opposed to CEO leadership, are still on the immature side," one experienced director observed. "Where something cathartic has happened—there have been life-threatening experiences, CEOs change, maybe new people have come onto the board—my sense and my experience is that [board activity is] more advanced, and people take it more to heart and tend to see the value of it."

When the board is seriously challenged, the need for information also becomes more acute, as another director explained: "I think there will be more demand for more information in particular areas when a company is being challenged. And the board members try to ask more insightful questions, to be supportive and helpful to management in making their decisions. I think we've been doing this well at [company name] because [the CEO] encourages it, but still we may have to put more pressure on him." As this comment indicates, reciprocal attentiveness to the emotions stirred up on both sides is another important aspect of the relationship between the board and management.

When directors set out to press management for more information, they report taking pains to do so tactfully and to communicate their continuing confidence in management. As one director recounted, "When [management] walked in and sat down around the edge of the room, I said, 'Folks, we're very aware of all the work you've done. We've had a great review of all that. But there is an enormous amount of information here. You all, we know, have made very significant decisions to get to the conclusions you've come to. We suspect they are the right decisions. But the only way we will know, and be able to put our judgment on that, is if you'll permit us the opportunity to test you in many ways during the next couple of days of discussions, so that we can get through the same small knotholes and decisions you did, in the same way that you did. And you're going to need to be patient with us, if you'll do that with us.' They did, we did, and we got to a very common ground. But it took a lot more intense discussion, and an environmental change between the management and the board that says asking questions, probing deeply, is not bad, it's good."

The same director described his delicate dealings with individual managers: "I go very close to the line, I know that. But seldom have I crossed the line where I said, 'Hey, Mike, I think you ought to do this,' or 'John, you ought to do that.' But I do constantly inquire of them what is going on. I cross off the input that I get from all the different places, and where it's not matching up right for me, I go back and say, 'Hey, this isn't fitting yet. John, this doesn't sound good. I think you ought to go look at this, because I'm concerned that you think this will happen and I'm concerned that this is what's really happening.' And I think that involvement is necessary. Look, I'm not smarter than the people that are managing this day to day. But I've got the benefit of not being burdened by having one hundred meetings on my calendar day to day, and I can take advantage of what it is I learned over forty years and then help them see things that are getting by them that they don't see just because they're on the playing field."

Yet another board member described what happens when a board lets the CEO dominate the discussion: "I think that what happens is you get this kind of groupthink on the board, where the CEO sets the agenda and after a while people stop objecting."

According to all these directors, what actually transpires in a boardroom depends not only on the role the board adopts, implicitly or explicitly, or on the understanding of the company the board gains. It also depends on how successfully the board builds a constructive relationship with management, especially the CEO.

Many directors emphasized that the board's relationship with management depends heavily on the leadership of the board itself. Although there have been many calls in recent years for American companies to separate the job of board chair from that of CEO, most of the companies whose directors we interviewed had gone a different route. They had created the position of lead director, typically occupied by an independent director, whose main job was to lead discussion when management was not present (see chapters 7 and 8).

As a number of our interviewees pointed out, selection of an effective lead director was important in improving management–board relationships. For one thing, a skilled lead director can ensure open communication with management. "I'm really happy that on all my boards we have a lead director who can be very blunt with the CEO," one director said. "And if people don't have a person like that on the board, or as part of the board structure, it must be set up." Another director expressed a similar perspective: "Lead director is an idea whose time really has come, and should come. It gives a focal point for the board and is a good information conduit. And board members who don't want to say to the CEO, 'Look, I think you're all wet on this idea' can tell the lead director."

The lead director, we were told, can also enable the CEO to raise sensitive issues with the board without damaging its relationship with him or her. "If you want the CEO to be transparent, . . . then you can't take every little thing that he tells you is wrong in the company and then drill down on it and beat him up on it. That's what gets management sometimes gun-shy about letting boards really know what's going on," one director said. "There's a role there for a lead director, to help the management and the communications between management and the board be totally transparent, but on the other hand not be abused."

Having a lead director, we were told, also helps boards deal with crises. When a board faces suddenly enhanced complexity and uncertainty, such a leader can help guide them. "Most people have lead directors now or presiding directors, or some such person. And I think that is one area that, in this crisis, had needed to be made a real job," one director told us. "And boards who do well in this crisis are ones that are well led. It's not just the naming of such a person, or presiding over [executive sessions]—it's much, much more than that."

The lead director typically works closely with the CEO on behalf of the board to ensure that the board's agendas include issues of importance to the board and that the board gets the information it wants. "Several directors say to the chairman of the governance committee, who might also be the lead director, . . . 'Look, we're concerned about this. Would you bring it up with management when you have your regular chat, and ask management to set aside some time at the next board meeting to discuss whatever the issue is?'" one director explained. "I think that might work. I don't think individual directors doing things is likely to work. But I think working through the governance committee or the lead director, . . . I think management would be responsive if it's done that way."[4]

## The Board's Activities

The directors pinpointed three activities that they believed their boards should address differently in the future: company strategy, management development and succession, and risk management. (Obviously missing from this list is compliance with laws and regulations; since passage of the Sarbanes-Oxley Act, and partly because of it, the directors believed that their boards were already handling these matters well.) When discussing these activities, the directors often related them to redefinition of the board's role.

**BOARD INVOLVEMENT IN STRATEGY.** The directors were clearly in agreement that the task of defining company strategy belongs to management; the board's job is testing, assessment, and approval (see chapter 2). As one director put it: "Boards really shouldn't be setting strategy—management should be setting the strategy. But, certainly, boards should be there to keep management honest, and to ask the right questions and to really figure out how we want to do it—appropriate milestones, appropriate questions, appropriate dashboard, to continue to monitor how things are going."

Another interviewee drew on experience to express a similar perspective: "In my experience, the strategy comes from management, not from the board. The board hears about the strategy, approves the strategy, insists that there *is* a strategy—but it is the management's strategy, not the board's strategy. The board approves it, like a lot of things, but in my experience I haven't seen a board craft a strategy."

Directors did have ideas about how the board might oversee strategy better. Several wanted to see the board press for a longer-term perspective in strategic planning. As one director said, "In terms of things that I think could be better, I still think—especially in this financial crisis—that the long-range planning tends to get put aside too much. And it's very hard to see really where we're going for more than about 90 to 120 days. We have plans and so forth, but I just think the long term—where are we going to be in the three-to-five-year range?—I think that is still not paid enough attention to."

Some interviewees disagreed on the grounds that, in a financial downturn of this magnitude and scope, boards ought to focus on the short term, particularly in the financial services industry. "At this time, there's a focus on understanding the nearer-term implications before returning to long-range planning," one said. "In fact, we actually decided that. We do a long-range strategic plan offsite every spring, and we decided that it really doesn't make sense for management to spend a lot of time between now and then trying to gin up another five-year plan or three-year plan, and they would be better off focusing on nearer term, and making sure that we see the opportunities in the near term. Because with any market dislocations like these, or economic dislocations, there are opportunities as well as risks, and so we really want them thinking about that."

Other directors argued that their boards ought to be more proactive in shaping discussions with management about strategy. "And so what I am starting to see at some boards is the board is being more proactive, and perhaps a bit more directive, about framing the strategy discussion," one director reported. "So what do I mean by that? Management may want to talk about a series of interesting new investments and initiatives as the centerpiece of their strategy discussion, but the board may want to talk about competition, relative performance, other issues like that. So I'm starting to see boards say, 'Let's look at an outline of how you, management, want to discuss the strategy.' And the nonexecutive chair, the lead director, would share that with the other directors and kind of solicit input. It would sometimes be face-to-face, sometimes by phone, and [they would] say, 'OK, does the strategy discussion that management is proposing fulfill your needs and answer your questions, or are there other topics that you want to talk about?' And that way, the board perhaps asserts more control over the direction and the composition of the strategy discussion, as opposed to what management solely wants to talk about."

A number of directors asserted that how a board involves itself in strategy ought to depend on the company's circumstances. One interviewee observed, for example, that boards' involvement in strategy should also depend on the experience and knowledge of the directors themselves: "Board role in strategy is going to vary a lot by industry and by director ability to contribute on the strategy side. So in a leading-edge, high-tech company, most directors are not going to understand the market, or the products or the technologies, well enough to play a substantive role in terms of contributing to strategy. The best they can do is make sure that management in its discussion and application of the strategy is internally consistent and is true to the things that they believe about market and strategy."

In sum, in spite of differences of opinion, these directors considered it critically important to ensure that management develops a strategy that the board can in turn assess and approve and that can serve as a template against which to judge company performance. They were also searching for better ways to do so.

**INVOLVEMENT IN MANAGEMENT SUCCESSION AND DEVELOP-MENT.** The directors to whom we spoke considered a successful CEO transition to be the board's critical responsibility (see chapter 3). "I think succession planning—thoughtful, careful succession planning—is critically important," one director said. "And not just at the juncture whereby succession needs to pass, but years in advance to make sure there is depth of understanding." Another director used McDonald's as an example to argue that boards should always have a ready supply of CEO candidates in-house: "I think a board should never be in a position where they have no candidates in-house for the CEO. The poster boy for really good board planning on management succession is McDonald's. Two guys die, and within eighteen months! Remember that? Heart attack, cancer. Each time, they had a guy ready to go, and they're doing fine now. Here you are, three CEOs in eighteen months, tragically, and the third guy, I think, is still in charge. That's the management succession that you need to be doing."

A number of directors acknowledged that their own boards need to improve their effectiveness in this arena. "I have some experience with that, as I've been brought into three CEO positions now from the outside," one said. "And what I found behind me upon arrival is a real dearth of detailed succession planning from the board." Another described efforts to avoid other companies' mistakes: "[Boards are] spending a lot of time on succession planning because we know a lot of companies haven't done a good job with that."

One director noted that one impediment to good succession planning is limited opportunity to expose up-and-coming managers to the board: "There are relatively few companies that have had the luxury, in this period of enormous growth and highly specialized activity, to broadly expose somebody through cycles to enough of what's going on that you'd be confident he or she could take the seat." A second director noted the difficulty of assessing how well the CEO who actually made the management-succession decisions was doing so: "How do we really evaluate the CEO, and, more importantly, what's the CEO's succession plan beyond just putting a book together and letting it gather dust on the shelf between meetings?"

Another director explained why boards tend to defer this issue: "I'd say to some extent with all three companies, now that we have relatively new CEOs, we're probably less into a succession-planning dialogue because, at least right now, there's nothing imminent on the horizon other than the proverbial get-hit-by-a-truck kind of problem. And the real issue is much more of really beginning to identify some potential leaders deeper in the organization."

Often, thinking about succession and management development was deferrable. In a context in which boards typically have more tasks than time, the board is understandably relieved when a set of issues can be deferred. Deferring the topic can be problematic, however, too often leading to time-pressured recruitment from the outside. And as has been pointed out, selecting successors from outside the company can be problematic and costly.[5]

RISK MANAGEMENT. Another activity uppermost in the thoughts of the directors was, unsurprisingly, risk management. They had witnessed other companies, and in some cases their own, fail to anticipate and control risk during the financial decline. One director spoke for many: "I think now there is more and more concern that risk has to be a board-level activity." Although there was consensus on this point, opinions varied about who should manage which risks. One point of view was that all risks, even broad business risks, are the responsibility of the audit committee. "I would say, yes, risk assessment is an area that has taken on a lot of importance over the last couple of years," one director told us. "I've seen it handled quite effectively within the context of the audit committee—raising that to a higher level of importance, perhaps, among the charter responsibilities—and, as you sort of calendarized the charter to figure out what you're going to do at each meeting, whether it's telephonic or face-to-face, I've seen and I've done it, because I chair the audit committee at [company name]. And we have raised the profile of risk assessment, particularly in the food industry, with all of the reputational issues that that could bring to you if somebody gets food poisoning because the cheese on the pizza isn't good."

An alternative point of view is that only boards facing substantial financial risk need a risk-management committee. "Just judging by what I'm reading and hearing, the knee jerk seems to be 'Let's create a risk committee and we got it done.' And I think that's appropriate for [a large bank]. I don't think it's appropriate for [manufacturing companies]," one director asserted. "I think it is a board-level, not committee-level, responsibility to go through the major risks—after all, they're supposed to be in the 10-K every year. Go through the major risks and how the company is managing them, and what oversight and where it should be provided at the board level."

Others insisted that the responsibility for risk management rests with the entire board because of the broad experience required. "I think a big part of that is to help the management assess risk," one director said. "It's one of the things that a good board can do, because of all the experiences around that table from various industries. They can also help a lot with identifying those so-called strategic risks . . . They may not know the business as well as the management, but they can certainly help identify risk outside the company."

Another director made essentially the same point in more detailed terms: "Enterprise risk management [ERM] evaluations are good, but they tend to be somewhat superficial. I think where risk really engages in a company is down, to some extent, in the weeds, and the ERM kind of flies over the canopy of the trees. I think that too much has been put on the audit committee to assess risk, and I think that's coming out of trying to fix yesterday's problem of controls and Sarbanes-Oxley. I think we're still focused there. So I think risk should be a component of every committee, and not owned by the audit committee. It should be more focused on financial and operating risk in addition to control risk."

Still other directors observed that boards are highly dependent on their CEOs for judging risk. "I think my lesson is that ERM only goes so far, and that in the end I almost think what we depend on as shareholders— I'm going to step back from being a director, and then we can go back into the director's chair—but as shareholders, with these big, complex companies that we have, what we almost depend on is that the CEO has an intuitive feel for risk," one director said. "It, sadly, can't all depend on oversight. But the directors are in a position to have a feel for the CEO's risk intuition. And in the end, that's a very valuable protective tool."

Many directors acknowledged that the prevailing preoccupation with risk is a reaction to recent events. "In this economy, I think, first, it has changed what the board is focusing on right now," one director said. "And I think the second thing that it's done has just so heightened the sense of risk, unknowability, and, frankly, vulnerability of any institution and the kinds of consequences that can come from decisions." Others considered it vitally important to take a longer-term and broader view of financial crises. "Now there's no excuse. Everybody—financial business or industrial business—has to have risk management as a much more important function, partly because energy is a derivative, a financial derivative," one seasoned director pointed out. "We were very fortunate just to watch the derivative risk five years ago, build a risk-management system, and now we're taking it from commodities and moving it to money, and then moving to do geopolitics, and trying to come up with enterprise risk understanding that I think is respectably advanced in its thinking. But it's because we started on this about five years ago."

Still other directors agreed that risk management is something that boards should always have concentrated on: "I think risk management in general has to be much more on the radar screen. And financial risk—even in how you manage your cash, how you manage your investments, pension funds and other things, if there is such a thing—and all those are going to have to be relooked at," one director said. "My sense is that a lot of management teams and boards gave lip service to risk, maybe looking at the more obvious risks. But I think the lesson of the last two years is [that] there are a lot of risks that we haven't really thought about and we need to consider."

These directors clearly believed that it ought to be a priority for their boards to focus on business risks, especially financial risks. However, they disagreed about how to do so, or about how doing so would mesh with their other activities. This uncertainty is unsurprising, since the magnitude of financial risks is a recent discovery for many boards. As often happens when an institution confronts a new set of issues, some of the directors' worries may turn out to be excessive, and those concerns that are valid will have to be addressed in a way that will not compromise other activities.

## What Was Not Said

When a study employs open-ended questions, as this one did, it is often informative to identify the topics that respondents rarely raised. This was a particularly interesting exercise in the case of these directors, who barely mentioned two matters high on the governance agendas of shareholders and the organizations that speak for them, as well as those in Washington, DC : executive compensation and the relationship between boards and shareholders.

Shareholders' most significant complaints about executive compensation are (1) that senior executives are paid too much, and (2) that their pay often seems unrelated to their own or their companies' performance; some CEOs who have performed poorly are even granted lump-sum payments on departure. The directors we spoke to were certainly aware of these objections, but less personally concerned about them than with the topics we have already discussed. We cannot be certain why this is so. One possibility is that the shareholders of their companies are not indignant about compensation. If so, these directors might see the debate about executive compensation as a matter of immediate concern to companies other than their own.

When we speak of the relationship between boards and shareholders, we refer to various attempts by shareholders and the organizations that represent them, and by regulators, to enhance shareholder influence over the companies whose shares they own. Some of these actions are intended to reform the election of directors, notably efforts to abolish staggered boards, to revise majority-voting rules, and to give shareholders access to the company proxy statement. Other shareholders are simply asking for more direct communication with the board.

Traditionally, boards have left such matters either to the company's legal staff, in the case of shareholder proposals, or to company executives (the CEO, the CFO, or the investor relations executive) in the case of communications. The underlying assumption is that it is preferable to let full-time employees speak for the company; there is more than a hint in this stance that executives, as well as many directors themselves, fear that part-time board members could prove ill-informed or undisciplined in communicating with shareholders. This mind-set may explain why even the experienced directors with whom we spoke did not consider the question a serious matter for their boards.

We believe, however, that these two issues must be confronted because of the Dodd-Frank bill and its ramifications—"say on pay" and the ongoing discussion about proxy access.

# The Key to Improving Boards

These intriguing omissions aside, what is most noteworthy in our interviews is the overall thrust of the directors' thoughts on what makes for effective boards. In their view, effectiveness has little to do with regulators, laws, recent shareholder initiatives to change board elections, and so on, and everything to do with what transpires within individual boards. The determinants that shape boards' behavior, in the eyes of our interviewees, are illustrated in figure 1-1. What really matters, they told us in a variety of ways, is for each board to achieve clarity about its role—that is, about the extent and nature of its involvement in strategy, management succession, risk oversight, and compliance.

This conception of the board's activities has several important implications. If, as our interviewees insisted, each board's effectiveness is directly attributable to its activities, it follows that boards

FIGURE 1-1

**Three interrelated issues**

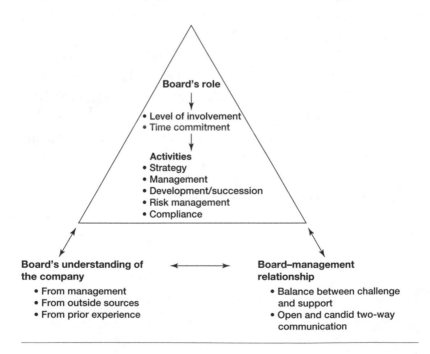

have a responsibility to define their own role with precision and to decide how to perform it in light of the nature of the firm, its management, its industry, and its particular challenges. To gain this understanding, boards will have to invest extended time in hard-headed discussions of both, leading to concrete and actionable conclusions.[6]

Whatever the choices a board makes about its role, they must be consistent with the members' shared understanding of their company. Furthermore, although legally the board wields the ultimate power in the corporate hierarchy, as a practical matter it can execute its role successfully only if it develops and maintains a sound relationship with management. Such a relationship calls for explicit agreement, on the part of the board and management, about the role of each in leadership of the company. It also requires open two-way communication and mutual respect between the two parties.

To be effective, in sum, boards have to maintain a delicate balance in their relationship with management. They must be challenging and critical on the one hand and supportive on the other. They have to sustain an open and candid flow of communication in both directions. They must also seek external sources of understanding outside management without offending management.

None of this is easy, but all of it is essential for effective governance. Failure to achieve any component of this prescription can undermine the effectiveness of the board, and ineffective boards have contributed to the corporate failings that have recently been far too conspicuous in the landscape of the American economy.

## Notes

1. The Corporate Governance Initiative has served since 1999 as a forum to discuss and encourage faculty research.

2. These interviews were conducted before the Dodd-Frank bill was enacted.

3. *Delaware General Corporation Code Annotated*, sec. 14(a), title 8, http://www.delcode.state.de.us.

4. For more about the board's relationship to its CEO, see Stephen Kaufman, "Evaluating the CEO," *Harvard Business Review*, October 2008.

5. For more about the board's role in management succession, see Joseph L. Bower, *The CEO Within: Why Inside Outsiders Are the Key to Succession Planning* (Boston: Harvard Business School Press, 2007); and Rakesh Khurana, *Searching for a Corporate Savior: The Irrational Quest for Charismatic CEOs* (Princeton, NJ: Princeton University Press, 2002).

6. For a complementary perspective, see Colin B. Carter and Jay W. Lorsch, *Back to the Drawing Board: Designing Corporate Boards for a Complex World* (Boston: Harvard Business School Press, 2004).

# Two

# Focusing on Strategy to Govern Effectively

KRISHNA PALEPU

As reported in the previous chapter, one of the most common and persistent frustrations for independent board members is that they feel insufficiently engaged with the critical strategic issues and business risks facing their companies. In a survey of public companies by *McKinsey Quarterly* conducted in February 2008, a vast majority of the directors answering said they spend only about 20 percent of their board time on strategic issues, and that they would like to increase significantly the amount of time they spend on strategy in the next two to three years.

Unfortunately, not much seems to have changed since then. In its latest survey of over 1,500 public company directors, McKinsey reported that the proportion of board time spent on strategy-related matters hardly increased between 2008 and 2011. In addition, even when board members are focused on a company's strategy, the survey results indicated that a significant proportion of boards passively review and approve management's proposed strategy rather than actively work with management in debating and developing the strategy. Finally, only about 20 percent of the directors in the survey felt that they had a complete understanding of their company's strategy, only 16 percent said that they completely understood how their company created value, and only 10 percent said that they had a complete grasp of their company's industry. Not surprisingly, about 70 percent of the board members who participated in the 2011 McKinsey survey felt that shifting more of their time and attention to strategy would be the most valuable activity over the next two to three years.[1]

Indeed, many companies have been paying considerable attention to recruiting high-quality board members with relevant skills and experience. However, based on many years of watching company boards, I believe that even boards with A-grade board members are vulnerable to performing at a below-A-grade level unless they are deeply engaged with their company's strategy. After all, none of the critical board functions—overseeing the strategy and resource allocation; hiring, compensating, and evaluating the company's CEO; overseeing the financial reporting—can be done effectively unless the board is deeply knowledgeable about the company's strategy. Yet, as survey after survey shows, it is challenging for outside directors to effectively engage with the strategies of the companies on whose boards they serve.

## Hewlett-Packard: Consequences of Neglecting Strategy

A great deal of my thinking about board engagement with strategy is influenced by three cases on the Hewlett-Packard Company (HP) that I wrote (along with coauthors) in the last decade. The first case involved the highly contentious decision in 2000 by the company's board to acquire Compaq.[a] This happened soon after the company replaced its CEO with Carly Fiorina, an outside hire. Fiorina was brought in with the explicit mandate to deal with the strategic challenge the company was facing as a result of fundamental changes in its industry. These decade-long changes, marked by the rise of Wintel platform–based PCs and servers, commoditized a significant part of HP's business. Whereas the company failed to respond to these changes during the 1990s, two of its key competitors developed innovative business models to deal with the same change. Treating commoditization as an opportunity, Dell created a low-cost, flexible business model. IBM, after its own struggles, responded by creating a service-based information technology solutions model. Because HP was "stuck in the middle," its performance languished (as did the performance of Compaq, which faced similar challenges). After a bitter boardroom struggle and an acrimonious proxy fight, HP's shareholders narrowly backed the board's decision to acquire Compaq. Less than two years after backing Fiorina on the Compaq deal, the board fired her in response to internal turmoil and disappointing post-merger performance.

After Fiorina was gone and another outside CEO, Mark Hurd, was hired, the boardroom drama continued.[b] The second case documents the continued bitter divisions in the boardroom regarding the future direction of the company. As the board struggled to resolve these divisions, unauthorized press leaks of sensitive boardroom discussions occurred. In response, the board conducted ill-conceived investigations into the leaks that turned out to be illegal. This, in turn, led to significant board turnover.

Although the company's financial performance improved for the next few years under Hurd's leadership, its strategic challenges remained unresolved. The third case revolves around the recent firing of Hurd and the hiring of another outside CEO, in the context of Hurd's ethical transgressions.[c] The subsequent turmoil led to the departure of four board members and the induction of five new directors. HP's board again mired itself in controversy, with observers and investors questioning the board's decisions and wondering about the future strategic direction of the company.

Although there are a number of reasons for the turmoil in HP's boardroom, it is clear that one of the root causes of the problem was that the company's board failed to address the strategic headwinds in its industry in a timely fashion. As the board struggled to catch up, it repeatedly found itself hiring a series of outside CEOs. It is reasonable to ask, Why did the board neglect the strategic challenges for so long? Was the CEO hiring process informed by a deep introspection about the company's strategic needs, or was it driven by a desire to attract star CEOs as potential saviors?

The three HP cases discussed here span a decade. During this time period, the composition of HP's board changed significantly. Throughout this period, all the individuals on HP's board were outstanding professionals with great accomplishments. Why did a group of A players—different groups at different times—end up with such challenging situations? Is this the price of not engaging with strategy at the right time in the right manner?

Although HP is a dramatic example, there are many great companies that have suffered strategic failures—Sears, General Motors, and Citigroup, just to name a few prominent examples. It is easy to point fingers at these companies' boards, ex post facto. Is there something that can be done to increase the odds that boards can do better?

a. Krishna Palepu and Jonathan Barnett, "Hewlett-Packard-Compaq: The Merger Decision," Case 104-048 (Boston: Harvard Business School, 2004).

b. Jay Lorsch, Krishna Palepu, Elliott Sherman, and Carin-Isabel Knoop, "Hewlett-Packard Co.: The War Within," Case 107-030 (Boston: Harvard Business School, 2006).

c. Jay Lorsch, Krishna Palepu, and Melissa Barton, "Hewlett-Packard Company: CEO Succession in 2010," Case 411-056 (Boston: Harvard Business School, 2010).

# The Challenge

Why is it that most directors, despite their interest in being strategically engaged, find it difficult to do so? I believe there are four critical barriers.

## *Lack of Role Clarity*

One of the most important barriers for board engagement in strategy, as pointed out in chapter 1, is a lack of clarity regarding exactly what role boards should play with respect to strategy. Many board members believe that their job is to select the CEO, and that it is the CEO's job to decide on a company's strategy. This view is based on the belief that CEOs, who have both the requisite industry expertise and time, are the most appropriate ones to do the appropriate analysis and choose a strategy. In this framework, the board's role is to approve the strategy and then monitor its execution.

Although there is a lot of merit to this perspective, there are two potential issues that call for a more expanded role of the board. First, how does a board select a CEO if it is not in a position to identify the company's strategic needs and challenges? In fact, one of the pitfalls of CEO selection, identified by Rakesh Khurana, is that many boards seem to gravitate toward appointing CEOs as "charismatic leaders," leading to a number of pathologies.[2] Second, if the board does not actively engage in the strategy formulation process, how can it exercise its responsibility, often stated clearly in board charters, of approving a company's strategy? And how can it effectively monitor the implementation if it does not fully grasp the underlying hypotheses and assumptions embedded in the strategy?

In my view, it is better to approach strategy as an area in which there is an overlap in responsibilities for both the CEO and the board. A good practice is to view this as a partnership in which both the board and management actively collaborate. Clearly, the CEO and the rest of the management team have the time and expertise to formulate a company strategy, but boards have to play an active role in debating the underlying assumptions and implications. At a minimum, this process will help the board understand the strategy deeply before it is approved, and in some instances, it will help management to modify the strategy proposed in the first round.

For a board to play a satisfactory role in strategy, the first step, therefore, is to clarify how its partnership with management in the strategy-setting process will work.

## Lack of Strategic Focus in Board Agendas

A second significant barrier for strategic engagement by a board is its own agenda. Although many boards say that they want to spend time on strategy, a careful look at their actual agendas shows that very little board time is in fact allocated to strategy. A majority of a board's meeting time is often allocated to financial and operating reviews and attending to compliance matters. This is not surprising given the current governance climate. First, board meetings often coincide with quarterly earnings announcements, and given Wall Street's focus on quarterly numbers, boards feel compelled to spend a lot of time reviewing the latest quarter's performance. Second, recent regulatory changes such as the Sarbanes-Oxley Act and the Dodd-Frank Act have significantly increased compliance oversight responsibilities. Third, increased shareholder activism is putting a spotlight on board processes in areas such as governance, compensation, and risk management. Committee work has become more time consuming, increasing the time allotted to committee reports to the full board.

Even though most boards have increased their time commitments, this time has been taken up by these regulatory and financial imperatives, with very little time left on board agendas for strategic matters. Even when boards spend some time on business updates, time is often taken up by lengthy presentations by management, with little opportunity for active discussion and debate. Additionally, the selection of the topics for business updates is often ad hoc, not driven by any overarching strategic logic.

Some boards address the lack of strategic focus in regular board meeting agendas by adding a special annual strategy retreat. This is definitely a step in the right direction. However, it is hard to integrate strategy into regular board work unless these annual retreats are closely connected to the agenda and discussions in every board meeting. Many annual strategy retreats are dominated by a discussion of five-year strategic plans and associated financial numbers, not a deep discussion of the company's industry, its competitors, and its core strategic value proposition for gaining competitive advantage.

## Lack of Strategic Information

The third, and probably most important impediment, is the typical board book. The thick binders that boards receive prior to every board meeting are often full of financial and operational information, but this often fails to inform boards adequately about the company's strategy and its execution. If directors receive information on the most pertinent set of strategic issues, they will be able to understand, monitor, question, and challenge the company strategy. Access to strategic information also facilitates better discussion in the boardroom and encourages more constructive questioning from the directors. In the absence of appropriate strategic information, it is difficult for board members to challenge management, or challenge other board members, in an objective and analytical manner.

How does a board elicit participation from directors who may have a nagging suspicion that the company is on the wrong track? In some cases, directors hesitate to raise an issue because they are not well versed in the industry or because they think that they are simply not seeing things correctly. Therefore, how does a board allow these issues to surface? Unless there is sound leadership in the boardroom—either an independent board chair or a strong lead director if the board chair is also the CEO—barriers to open and frank discussion of strategic dilemmas facing a company can develop. This is particularly true when a company has had a run of strong performance results but there are significant industry changes that might require the company to challenge itself to renew itself and pursue a different direction.

## A Framework for Strategic Engagement

Whereas directors are confronted with these numerous barriers, they often join a company's board because they would like to contribute to the strategic direction of the company. What is the best way to go about doing this? An easy recommendation would be to urge directors to spend more time on board work. However, given that most board members have already significantly increased their time commitment, this is not practical, unless we make board membership a near-full-time job.

Another seemingly obvious alternative is to recommend that all board members should have a deep background and experience in the industry. This too is impractical for several obvious reasons. First, current independence requirements make it very difficult to identify potential board members within the industry who do not run afoul of potential conflicts. Second, even if one could create a board full of industry experts, it is not clear that this is necessarily a good idea. Today, boundaries are blurring across industries, and globalization and new technologies are giving rise to dramatically new business models. A board consisting of some industry experts but also some industry outsiders with horizontal thinking capabilities is more likely to spot and respond effectively to potential disruptive changes on the horizon. Third, increased compliance requirements on audit and compensation committees are making it necessary to recruit technical specialists with relevant expertise, whether or not they have relevant industry experience. So, realistically, altering board composition, while potentially helpful, is unlikely to be a panacea for increased strategic engagement.

In my view, a practical and sustainable approach to enhanced strategic engagement will focus on increasing the return on time being already spent by board members, rather than asking them to spend more time on their board work. It also should facilitate engagement by board members who do not necessarily have a deep background in the company's industry, not just those with industry expertise. Finally, the approach should integrate strategic engagement with the general board work. With these criteria in mind, I propose the following framework.

### Step 1. Understanding Strategy: Four Questions That Every Board Should Ask

One of the most important reasons many board members feel that it is challenging to fully understand their company's strategy is because strategy presentations to boards often consist of endless PowerPoint presentations with a lot of jargon and unnecessary complexity. I have a simple prescription to address this: ask your management to provide short answers in plain language to the following four key questions. In my experience, if you know the answers to these questions at an intuitive level, as a board member, you can be confident that you understand the essence of your company's strategy.[3]

1. *What does the customer we are targeting need and what is our proposed solution?*
   The customer, not the company, is the right starting point for strategic thinking. Without satisfying a significant

customer need, no company can hope to be in business for long. Boards should have a clear sense of the unmet customer need(s) that their company is seeking to target and satisfy. The more clearly articulated the customer segment and its need is, the easier it is to understand and assess the nature of the business opportunity the company is pursuing, the potential for growth and profitability, the capabilities the company must have to address the customer need, and the nature of the competition it is likely to face in the marketplace. Strategic failures often occur when companies try to be all things to all customers and, in the process, fail to solve any particular customer segment's need optimally. Failures also often occur when companies target customer needs that they assume exist, or solutions that they assume address the customer needs, but customers either do not feel the need or the company's offer does not address their real need.

2. *Who are our competitors and how do we win against them?*
   In a free market economy, any meaningful customer need is unlikely to be targeted by just one company. Customers often have several offerings from which to choose, so it is important for boards to have a clear sense of the competitive landscape in which the company operates. Who are the relevant competitors? How are the competitors solving the customer's problem? What is the fundamental basis on which we expect to differentiate our offering from competitors' offerings—features, service, or brand image? Do customers value our differentiation? If customers cannot differentiate between our offering and those of competitors, or if customers do not value our difference, then the only basis on which we can compete and win in the market will be based on price—in other words, we become a commodity. And everyone knows how challenging it is to make money in a commodity world.

3. *What do we need to do to make our strategy profitable?*
   A sound customer value proposition is necessary, but not

sufficient, to make a strategy profitable. There are many examples of companies that create a lot of value for their customers but struggle to make money. A company's profitability is simply a function of the price it can charge and the costs it has to incur to deliver value to its customers. Price is a function of how unique and valuable the product or service is to the customer. Costs are influenced by necessary expenditures a company needs to incur to create the capabilities and processes to deliver its unique value proposition. Whereas price is influenced by competition and customers' willingness to pay, costs are influenced by the nature of the company's relationship with its suppliers and how complex its value chain has to be to deliver its value proposition. Another factor that often influences a company's value to the customers, and hence its profitability, is its relationship with any companies in its ecosystem that might provide products and services to its customers that complement its value proposition.

Whether or not a strategy leads to profitability, at least in theory, is therefore a function of several factors. Some of these factors are determined by how a company is situated in its business ecosystem—its relationship with its customers, competitors, key suppliers, and complementors—and some of these factors are determined by the key organizational and technical capabilities a company needs to invest in to achieve its differentiation. Board members need to have a clear sense of these key strategic factors to assure themselves that their company's strategy is likely to be a *profitable* strategy.

4. *What is the game plan for sustaining our competitive advantage or for strategic renewal?*
   If your company has a winning strategy today, this does not guarantee that this strategy will be a winner tomorrow. One of the greatest business risks facing a company is that, as the world changes around it, it does not remain

vigilant and renew itself to retain its competitive edge. Threats to a company's competitive position emerge from many different sources. Customer tastes and needs change over time. Competitors will figure out a way to imitate what you do uniquely and to reduce or eliminate your differentiation. New business models using innovative new technologies provide compelling alternative solutions to your customers. Globalization brings in a host of new competitors that provide good enough solutions to your customers at a significantly lower price. Many great companies of yesterday are no longer around today as a result of their inability to foresee or respond to these types of changes. Therefore, boards must have a continual discussion about potential strategic threats and how the company's strategy will adjust to changes in the marketplace.

Boards interested in being strategically engaged should ask their CEO and top management to provide simple and short answers to these questions. In my view, it is the board's job to ask these questions. The company's CEO and management team have the responsibility for proposing the answers. A process of interaction between the board and management will then lead to final answers that are satisfactory both to the board and to management.

### Step 2. Monitoring Strategy Execution

Boards do plenty of performance monitoring, so how exactly is it different from monitoring strategy? To understand the difference, consider figure 2-1. For a strategy to lead to desired financial outcomes, a company needs to continuously monitor whether or not it is continuing to invest in and nurture the key capabilities and processes; whether or not these capabilities and processes are being applied to deliver the proposition that was promised to the customers; and whether or not the net financial consequences of both these activities result in sufficient profitability over the long term to meet or exceed investor expectations.

FIGURE 2-1

## From strategy to profits

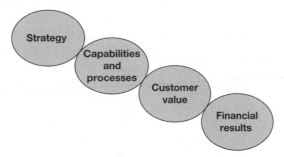

*Source:* This approach is a variation of the balanced scorecard framework developed by Robert Kaplan and David Norton. See Robert Kaplan and David Norton, "The Balanced Scorecard: Measures That Drive Performance," *Harvard Business Review*, January–February 1992.

Although boards may discuss their strategy in their annual board retreats, the quarterly board meetings often focus mostly on short-term financial results As a result, boards often fail to monitor the vital intermediate steps—capability creation and delivering the customer proposition—on a routine basis. This failure can have serious consequences. Boards may make resource allocation decisions—including major acquisitions—without a deep connection to the overall strategy; they can put pressure on management to deliver short-term financial results, rather than focus on long-term strategic success; and they may not ensure that the company's financial performance is communicated to investors in the context of the company's strategy, leading investors to focus on short-term results.

One way to make sure that a company's board integrates strategy into its monitoring function is to (1) use the annual board retreat to set the year's strategic agenda, (2) use a board strategic information system to get regular information on the progress on this agenda, and (3) design a quarterly meeting agenda to monitor and discuss it.

1. *Use the annual board retreat to set the company's strategic agenda.* Annual board retreats can be a powerful mechanism through which a board can agree with management on the year's strategic agenda. A company's strategy, which by definition is a long-term vision to create value, is unlikely to change every year. However, even when a company's strategy is working

well, it is useful to review it annually to see whether it needs to be modified in any way, given industry changes.

Even when a strategy does not require any significant modification, there may be a need for strategic initiatives to execute the strategy better. For example, there may be new challenges or opportunities facing the industry or the company, such as dealing with an emerging competitor with an innovative business model that threatens to disrupt the industry, an opportunity to expand to a new geographic market, or a need to improve the company's innovation capacity. These discussions would lead to identification of new strategic initiatives that need to be undertaken or accelerating the initiatives already in place.

2. *Include a strategic information brief in every board book.*
   To monitor the strategic initiatives identified during a board retreat, boards need to receive regular updates. One useful way to accomplish this is to create a strategic information brief that accompanies each board book. In my own work with boards, I have found a simple design of the following kind works very well:

   - A "one pager" providing brief answers to the four strategic questions outlined earlier. This document essentially reiterates the company's agreed-upon strategy and makes sure that both the management and the board keep it in mind as they meet each quarter to discuss the company's progress and performance. The term *one pager* is intended to remind everyone that brevity and simplicity are essential for effective communication at the board level.

   - A "one pager" on each of the strategic initiatives identified at that year's annual retreat as part of the strategic agenda. This document provides a progress report, using agreed-upon metrics and milestones that track the initiative's implementation. The metrics can either be financial or nonfinancial, qualitative or quantitative. Once again, the key requirement is brevity and simplicity.

- A "one pager" on new developments regarding the company's customers and competition. This document is intended to ensure that the board is constantly informed about any important industry developments that might pose strategic risks and need board attention. In my experience, board books often contain very little information about customers and competition, so this document is meant to correct this bias.

3. *Use the regular board meetings to update on strategic issues.* The final piece in continual strategic engagement is to modify board agendas to create the space in every board meeting in which to discuss strategic matters. In every board meeting, the agenda should allocate sufficient time to review and discuss the updates on strategic initiatives. In addition, it would be useful to create a board calendar for discussing one aspect of the key strategic dimensions in each of the board meetings: customers, competition, key differentiation capabilities, and key strategic risks. This will ensure that the board is able to drill down into these key areas throughout the year and be ready for the following year's strategic engagement. Prescheduling these topics in the board's annual agenda in a predictable manner allows adequate preparation by management and the board to discuss these topics without fail during the year.

It is common for boards to begin their meetings with a review and discussion of the latest financial statements and to schedule the business presentations for a later time on the agenda. My recommendation is that board meetings begin with a strategy update and discussion. This ensures that sufficient high-quality time is spent on this important issue. It also allows the board to approach the financial discussion in the context of the strategic picture.

It is also important to integrate the strategic engagement with committee work, as well as with making major board decisions. For example, CEO compensation and CEO annual evaluation should at least in part be tied to the accomplishment of the strategic agenda. When a CEO is to be replaced, the board should use its strategic knowledge to find a candidate who best fits the strategic needs of the company. When major resource allocation decisions are to be made, the board should ask whether these plans help push forward the company's strategic agenda. The audit committee should make sure that the company's financial statements—key accrual estimates, footnotes, and management discussion and analysis—faithfully reflect the company's strategy and risks. Finally, in conducting the board evaluation, the nominating and governance committee should assess how effective the board is in its strategic engagement.

## Potential Payoff and Implementation

When boards follow this strategic engagement framework, they avoid the risk of following in the footsteps of the HP board described earlier. Instead, directors are actively engaged in the company's strategy and are able to identify problems early on so that they can be discussed and corrected on a timely basis. In addition, they are able to prioritize their responsibilities to effectively use their limited amount of time. Finally, the board's conversation can shift from discussions about tactical and financial data to the implementation of strategy and the environment within which the company operates.

## Notes

1. "Governance Since the Economic Crisis: McKinsey Global Survey Results," *McKinsey Quarterly*, July 2011.

2. Rakesh Khurana, *Searching for a Corporate Savior: The Irrational Quest for Charismatic CEOs* (Princeton, NJ: Princeton University Press, 2002).

3. For an excellent discussion of strategy, see Michael Porter, "What Is Strategy?" *Harvard Business Review*, November–December 1996.

# Three

# Managing Your CEO's Succession

## *The Challenge Facing Your Board*

JOSEPH L. BOWER

In most major industrial countries of the world, corporate law assigns the job of selecting the chief executive officer of a company to the board of directors. This legal responsibility is mirrored in much recent discussion by leading commentators on corporate governance, such as Jay Lorsch.[1] Indeed, it has become common in circles devoted to "good governance" to hear arguments that the management of CEO succession is the board's prerogative.

The objective of this chapter is to explain why the board's role in succession, though very important, must be distinctly subordinate

Previously published in *Boardroom Realities: Building Leaders Across Your Board*, edited by Jay A. Conger, ISBN: 978-0-470-39178-5, published by Jossey-Bass, copyright 2009 by John Wiley & Sons, Inc., 253–275.

to the role played by the incumbent chief executive if the board is to be effective. As important as CEO succession should be in the work of the board, the management of the succession process is one of the core responsibilities of the *incumbent top leadership.* The board is not constituted so that it can substitute for the CEO in the critical work of developing candidates or in making the final selection. In the case of large publicly held corporations, if the board is actually and not just formally choosing the CEO, it is usually a sign that the succession process has failed. The CEO did not do his or her job. Beyond describing the board's role, this chapter makes clear both how a constructive succession process can be managed and what the positive contribution is that the board can make to that process.

To make this argument, I draw upon my research on CEO succession, on case studies that illustrate that process, and on my own experience as a board member taking part in the succession process.[2]

Before beginning a discussion of the role of the board, a little context is useful. A capsule summary of recent research on the management and performance of major companies includes the following points.

- With few exceptions, the economic performance of publicly held corporations rarely exceeds the mean for long periods of time. Only a handful of companies have maintained performance that has kept them in the top quartile for more than a decade. Generally, high performers regress to the mean. A study of eighty-seven high performers in the 1976–1993 period showed a decline in spread above the Standard & Poor's (S&P) average from 21 percent to 2 percent.[3] Low performers rise toward the mean or disappear. The implication of these numbers is daunting. If performance prior to your CEO's arrival was above average, he or she will have to do something special to avoid a decline. If it was below average, your successor CEO will have a lot of problems to find and fix. Either way, the CEO has a very demanding job.

- If anything, the job has become more difficult. Accelerating technological change and globalizing markets have intensified competition. Growing, vast, and liquid capital markets have led to the emergence of an active market for corporate control. Companies that do not perform well are often gobbled up by strategic competitors or private equity funds. Top managements operate under enormous pressure.[4]

- Moreover, increasingly competitive global markets mean that world-class efficiency, capability for innovation, and customer focus are needed for sustained success. To achieve these capabilities, continuity in CEO leadership is critical.[5]

- One constant factor in the mix of attributes associated with those companies that sustain high performance over time is that they manage succession well. More often than not, they pick insiders to succeed incumbents.[6]

- My research shows that from a sample of 1,800 transitions, CEOs chosen from inside the organization perform better than outsiders whether or not the company has been doing well (table 3-1). The difference is less dramatic when performance prior to succession has been good.

- Careful case-by-case analysis of succession suggests that the reasons for this difference in performance have to do with the insider CEO's knowledge of the company's technologies, operations, and competitors as well as his or her knowledge of company capabilities and culture.[7]

- Despite the apparent superior performance of CEOs appointed from the inside and the importance of continuity, and in the face of the growing demands on leadership and the complexity of modern companies, CEO turnover is higher in this decade than in earlier times, as is the number of outsiders chosen as new CEOs.[8] Data from Booz Allen Hamilton's most recent study show *outsiders* replacing incumbents around 20 percent of the time, even though performance is consistently poorer and tenure shorter.

**TABLE 3-1**

### Median market-adjusted stock returns three years after the CEO change

| New CEO was an | Prior company performance was | |
|---|---|---|
| | Better than S&P 500 | Worse than S&P 500 |
| Insider | –3.4% | 4.5% |
| Outsider | –5.0% | –1.3% |

*Source*: Joseph L. Bower, *The CEO Within* (Boston: Harvard Business School Press, 2007), 13.

Taken together, the preceding points suggest that we are in a CEO succession crisis. Why? How could it be that the succession process is not working well when so many companies say that people are their most important asset and when succession is highlighted as a key board responsibility?

## The Challenges of CEO Succession

The answer has three parts, one touched on in the preceding section. These three parts provide the basis for understanding what role the board can and should play in CEO succession. First, the job of the CEO is very hard and probably has become harder in the last couple of decades. Second, the process of developing great candidates for leadership is demanding and time intensive, especially for the CEO. Third, the board is under a great deal of pressure to make a defensible choice of candidate. The chapter deals with each of these challenges in turn.

### The Job of CEO

Probably the most elegant and concise description of the CEO's job was provided by Ken Andrews in the opening chapter of his seminal work, *The Concept of Corporate Strategy*.[9] He parses the job into four basic tasks.

> Chief executives, presidents, . . . are first and probably
> least pleasantly persons who are responsible for the results
> attained in the present as designated by plans made
> previously. Nothing that we will say . . . can gainsay this
> immediate truth.

This is why, as a rule, CEOs are thought of as doing a good job during times of economic prosperity and performing badly during recessions. Executives have to own their results. Continuing, he suggests that CEOs see as their second principal function the creative maintenance and development of organizational capability that makes achievement possible.

In other words, they have to deploy the organization's resources in such a way that this builds the organization's capacities. The business of enterprise software provider SAP, for example, consists largely of building integrated reporting systems so that the many parts of large companies can be coordinated in a global strategic effort. Without such systems, global competitors are doomed to regionally fragmented activity. This activity leads in turn to a third key function:

> The integration of the specialist functions which enable their
> organizations to perform the technical tasks in marketing,
> finance, . . . which proliferate as technology develops and tends
> to lead the company in all directions. If this coordination is
> successful . . . , general managers will probably have performed
> the task of getting organizations to accept and order priorities
> in accordance with the company's objectives. Securing commit-
> ment to purpose is a central function of the president as organi-
> zational leader.

This is General Management 101. Nonetheless, it is still normal to find functional divisions of a company pursuing their own objectives. Thus a country manager of a commercial operation works to keep capacity employed and local customers satisfied, often at the expense of the programmatic needs of global customers of strategic importance as viewed from headquarters.

Finally, and most critical to the long-term future of the company, Andrews turns to the question of corporate purpose, the motivation for the entire idea of corporate strategy.

> The most difficult role . . . of the chief executive of any organization is the one in which he serves as the custodian of corporate objectives . . . The presidential functions involved include establishing or presiding over the goal-setting and resource allocation processes of the company, making or ratifying choices among strategic alternatives, and clarifying and defending the goals of the company against external attack or internal erosion.

To recap, regardless of who planned the action and who made the decisions leading to the present results, the CEO is responsible for current operations. That is why we ceremonially dispatch CEOs for the sins of their predecessors. Charles Prince was the general counsel of Citicorp. Because of a series of ethical lapses that led to large fines and the near shutdown of some important Citicorp operations in Europe and Japan, Prince was asked to succeed Sandy Weill and clean up the company. Three years later, he was fired for the severe consequences to Citicorp of their large subprime mortgage portfolio. Was it Prince's fault? It really doesn't matter. It happened on his watch. Unless a crisis is clearly pinned to the coattails of the previous CEO, its consequences belong to the incumbent.

In turn, the CEO has to build the organizational capabilities required to move forward. This will always require integrating the functional and strategic capabilities of the company. It is very clear that Prince was focused on compliance in his early moves. It is less clear that he focused on risk management. A fascinating positive example is provided by Sam Palmisano's work at IBM in transforming the company into a fast-moving, technologically creative provider of advanced IT solutions. The knitting together of IBM's global technological and commercial capabilities is remarkable.[10]

Finally, the CEO must preside over the crafting of corporate strategy, always a difficult task but now even harder because of the rapid change in market and environmental conditions. The CEO of

Nokia, Olli-Pekka Kallasvuo, recently remarked, "Who would have thought eighteen months ago that our most important challenge would come from Apple?"[11]

As this comment suggests, today's CEO has to operate, build organizational capability, and craft strategy in a world in which markets are global, new competitors based in a variety of economies—some state sponsored—emerge regularly, and technologies are evolving rapidly, thereby changing the basis of competitive advantage. And should the financial markets' judgment as to the company's prospects turn sour, a pool of close to two trillion dollars of liquid capital exists populated by fund managers ready to exploit a low share price with a contest for corporate control.

But the job of the successor CEO is even harder. The entire question of corporate objectives needs to be rethought, taking into account the circumstances of markets and technologies to come— not just the ones that the incumbent has been considering. Jack Welch most famously sold off the major acquisition of his predecessor, restructured the company so as to eliminate large staffs that the predecessor had built, and reoriented GE away from its industrial heritage in the United States and instead built major foreign operations and a financial services group of formidable strength. The results were remarkable. In contrast, Sir Richard Greenbury improved the efficiency of Marks & Spencer but made no fundamental change in its sourcing operation, so that the company was vulnerable to new kinds of mid-market retailing. The eventual result was a significant decline in financial performance. Under these circumstances, filling the shoes of CEO is no easy task. Where does one find such an unusual person?

## Developing CEO Candidates

I have already suggested that the best place to look is inside. This is such an obvious answer that one immediately is forced to ask, "Sure, but then why are there so many outsider CEO candidates?" In my study of over eighteen hundred transitions, a third of the new CEOs were outsiders.[12]

Here there are two parts to the answer. First, for a surprising but understandable set of reasons, many companies do a poor job of developing insiders who might arguably do an effective job of leading the company. Companies (more specifically the CEO and board of the company) are often forced to go outside. The basic reason is that they do not invest systematically in the development of leaders. One survey showed that 60 percent of the companies surveyed do not even have a succession planning process in place.[13] This number is so startling that it is often challenged when I speak to groups of managers. Yet when I poll the group, the number who think their company has a CEO succession planning process in place has never exceeded 40 percent and is often lower.

Many companies think a horse race among potential candidates is all you need to pick a winner, without worrying whether the horses are fast enough for the decade to come. These are companies that pride themselves on being obsessive about managing for performance, on paying and promoting those who deliver while firing those who don't. They deliver on plans without fail. But often they turn out to be companies that think investing resources to develop general managers is a waste of time, that human resources is a routine administrative function to be delegated and then ignored, and that CEO succession is something that you begin to worry about the year before the CEO retires. After describing to me the extensive arrangements that his high-performing company made for developing leaders at all levels, its CEO noted, "These are the expenses a financial buyer would strip out in an instant." In my discussions with the customers for executive programs at Harvard Business School, I am often told that our seven- and eight-week comprehensive general management programs take too much time. The customer then asks, "Can't you provide a transforming experience that takes three days?" When I reported this in a conversation with past GE CEO Jack Welch, he replied, "Joe, you've hit the nail on the head. That is exactly what I hear as I go around the country."[14]

But second, when many CEOs and their boards finally turn to succession, they may have a bias against the insiders. If there has been great success, it is easy for a view to develop that "the demands of our scale and scope are more than any of our people can handle. They haven't grown with the company." Of course this suggests that the company has not invested in that growth. In a similar vein, an "imperial" CEO may believe that "none of my people are up to my standard." Many CEOs who think that way have created a self-fulfilling prophecy. Most problematic, the insiders that have posted good performance sometimes seem to lack strategic vision. Unless they have been properly challenged with strategic assignments, they are "inside the box" operators. They do not understand the need for change.

My guess is that this weakness of insiders is the primary reason that performance of top-quartile companies regresses to the mean following succession. The new CEO does not really understand how much change is needed.

There are also more human reasons for picking outsiders. Some CEOs find the prospect of succession downright depressing. For them, succession implies a kind of personal "death." Their life is their job. They love the job; it is their identity. They are dead without it. They think of building a cohort of potential leaders not as the path to growth and prosperity but as a sure route to lame-duck status. Even among those who plan for succession, some manage in such an imperial fashion that the potential successor leaders wither in their shade. Sadly, some sitting CEOs in their heart of hearts fear being surpassed. A symptom of this problem is the CEO who values loyalty above competence. One of the executives I interviewed for my study put it this way:

> I've seen situations where people with the title CEO are insecure in their position. And, sometimes, times are difficult. The company isn't doing well. News of problems for the CEO usually comes from below, so the CEO may focus on loyalty, rather than who is the best candidate for the job. They want to know "who's watching my back?" . . . But the organization sees it. . . . And they start thinking, "Maybe this *isn't* a meritocracy."[15]

## When the Board Makes the Succession Choice

We can begin to understand the problem the board faces when it does put succession on its agenda. Let's summarize the problematic behaviors described earlier:

- Attention to short-term performance has been all that counted for promotions.

- The organization has been designed so that general management jobs are broken up into functional assignments, and candidates have never had the experience of running a whole business.

- General managers have not been developed with strategic assignments.

- CEO succession has been treated as an event, and discussion of that event has been awkward or postponed.

- The incumbent CEO has managed in an imperial fashion so that the top management cohort has never really developed their capabilities.

Where several of these behaviors are the norm, the board will find a cohort of operators as opposed to leaders when they turn to consider CEO succession. The men and women who have been described as performing at a high level are found to be lacking when measured against the criteria developed for the company's next leader. In particular, they do not see the need for real strategic change.

It is not surprising that when talent development has not been a priority of the company and its board, the board turns to outsiders. If performance has been poor, a natural reaction is that the insiders are part of the problem, not a source of the solution. It may be true. Unless the company's organization permits several managers to have the experience of running business units, it is hard to sort out the insiders who have not been unsuccessful. Outsiders bring a fresh view and an attractive track record.

Where performance has been good, it is not unusual for the incumbent CEO to frame the problem of succession as a choice among some number of his or her direct reports. Unless the board has been actively engaged in monitoring a talent development process, it is quite natural for the board to accept this assessment and discuss how the baton should be passed to the best of the candidates, or as a horse race managed among them. That is what happened at Marks & Spencer, where the winner of a horse race turned out to be considerably less than the job required. Faced with a very difficult retail environment, the new CEO Peter Salsbury panicked and made a series of poor moves that worsened the financial squeeze on the company. The board then brought in an outsider who managed a temporary turnaround. When that turned sour, the board finally brought in Stuart Rose, an insider who had left the company in frustration a decade earlier. Rose was able to rebuild Marks & Spencer's fundamental capabilities.

Let us consider the problem from the board's perspective. What happens when a board has been able to get involved and decides that the candidates are not up to the challenge? What if performance has not been good, and there is not a lot of faith in the recommendation of the incumbent? The problem, of course, is that a board, even a diligent board, is made up of part-timers whose knowledge of the company is based on what they have been presented at board meetings and whatever else they are able to gather from outside sources. Especially when performance has been problematic, there will be skepticism toward insiders.

To begin, it takes time to decide to act. If succession has not been a priority of the board for a period of time, the board will be reluctant to move unless there is a crisis. The 2007 study of succession by Booz Allen Hamilton found that CEOs who had experienced an absolute loss of shareholder value over two years of 25 percent or more and underperformed their regional peers by 45 percent were most likely to be removed. But the likelihood was only 5.7 percent. In discussion with the authors, we observed that boards without choices find it very hard to make a move![16] (See figure 3-1.)

FIGURE 3-1

## Termination and extreme performance

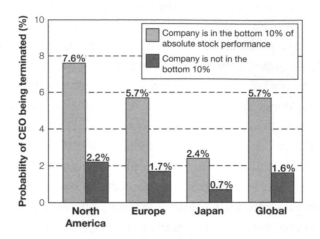

*Note*: Data does not include interim CEOs or merger-related departures.
*Source*: P. O. Karlsson, G. L. Neilson, and J. C. Webster, "CEO Sucession: The Performance Paradox," *strategy + business*, no. 51 (Summer 2008).

It is hard for directors to remove a CEO if they are not confident that inside successors are qualified. Inevitably, a board will turn to a search firm for assistance in assessing inside candidates and finding outsiders. Known colloquially as "headhunters," search firms play a crucial role in helping boards find new outsider CEOs. An important asset that these executive recruiters bring to the task is a database of executives who might be appropriate and available for the new job. Because search firms are a third party, they are able to begin a process of exploration under conditions of confidentiality, important both to the company and the candidates—because the candidates are usually employed somewhere else.

The forces at work as a board seeks an outsider have been well described by the sociologist Rakesh Khurana.[17] Central to what happens is concern for the credibility of the candidate and the due care taken by the board in the process. The members of a board seek to work collegially. As well, they are concerned that their decisions are defensible. The recommendation of a leading search firm of a candidate with a record of success at a well-known company counts for a great deal. It makes it easier for the board both to coalesce behind a candidate and to justify its decision.

Often the desire by a superficially informed board for credentials leads their search firm to find a celebrity CEO, a star from one of the "people factories" such as GE or Procter & Gamble.[18] For a board worried about declining performance or facing a crisis, celebrity CEOs provide the same kind of comfort that used to reassure purchasers of mainframe computers when they bought IBM. Unfortunately, it is not unusual for these very capable recruits to lack critical understanding of the companies' industries and markets. Examples of this sort would include PepsiCo's John Sculley, who moved from a stellar performance in the Cola Wars to Apple Computer, where he could not cope with Microsoft and Intel, and GE's Larry Johnson, who went from running GE's Home Appliance group well to running the Canadian retailer Albertson's poorly. But even when the outside recruit has the requisite knowledge of the business to lead the development of new strategy, he or she very often lacks the understanding of the company's culture and people needed to drive change. That would appear to have been the problem at 3M, where the brilliant James McNerney appears to have been unable to build on the firm's culture of creative innovation.

There is a second aspect to the outsider's problem. Many outsider CEOs who are brought in to turn around or reenergize a company are generalists who know how to drive efficiency but are fundamentally unequipped with the industry or market knowledge necessary to craft and implement an innovative strategy. They can cut costs but cannot drive growth. When they leave (the 2006 Booz Allen Hamilton succession study says three years is the reported average tenure for turnaround artists), profits may be better but the company is strategically weaker.[19] And their turnaround has not involved investment in leaders for the future. As a result, there are no potential CEOs within the organization. Of more concern, the same Booz Allen Hamilton study reveals that one-third of the time, the outsider CEO sells the company. Indeed there are CEOs who have made a serial business of such short turnarounds followed by a sale.

My research suggests that the answer to the dilemma posed by the problems of insiders and outsiders is what I call the *inside-outsiders*.

These are men and women who have performed well and risen high but have maintained their objectivity. Blessed with independent minds and high integrity, they have also been nurtured by executives who valued their capabilities and helped them learn to use them. They are aware of how much change is needed to sustain success or turn around a failure, but they also know the organization, its culture, and its people. They have learned to deliver on their commitments, so their track record is solid, but they have also been given the opportunity to drive strategic growth. They can do more than bring in consultants or make across-the-board cuts. Beyond getting short-term profits, they can build for future growth.

These unusual folk are often found at the periphery of the organization, managing new businesses or new markets. Among the well-known versions of this type are GE's Jack Welch, who rose to CEO from his role as maverick president of GE's Plastics group and transformed GE's culture and systems; his successor, Jeff Immelt, the first GE leader to come from sales, who dramatically increased the scale and potential of GE's medical system business (far from the core engine and turbine businesses); Procter & Gamble's A. G. Lafley, who came up in the personal care business and spent years building a very successful Far Eastern business (far from laundry and Cincinnati); and IBM's Sam Palmisano, who in a company known for closed systems and hardware championed open systems and software.

## Managing the Succession Process

Although I have argued the importance of building a cohort of inside-outsiders, it is obvious that much of the time boards are not faced with that prospect. We need, therefore, to consider both succession circumstances: incumbent to insider and incumbent to outsider.

### Incumbent to Insider

Well-managed succession is a process that meets at least three tests. Through their assignments, their evaluations, and their mentoring, executives grow to be effective leaders so that there is a pool of candidates for CEO to consider. That work is done by top management. All the board can do is to make sure it is happening. In the process of pruning the pool, as discussed earlier, the CEO and board need to have established criteria that reflect the needs of the company going ahead. In making their selection, they focus on values, intellectual integrity, and fit with future needs, as well as past performance. In today's fast-changing world, the past is not necessarily prologue.

Building a pool of leaders begins with recruitment to the company. It continues with a pattern of assignments that permits development of real expertise in a line of business and development of managerial skills. For that to happen, staffing needs to balance the needs of the businesses with the needs of the managers. A strong HR staff led by an executive who has the complete trust and commitment of the CEO is what it takes to make that happen. Evaluation and compensation are critical as well. Finally, planning and budgeting have to be managed with care so that it is a process in which managers grow, not a game of "gotcha" in which they succeed or fail on the basis of meeting short-term performance targets.

This takes time and discussion, often one-on-one with mentoring or coaching. Managers have to learn that accountability for one's commitments is critical to success in an organization. But because the future is uncertain, they have to learn that fast action in response to changed circumstances is an important aspect of producing on commitments. Finally, when proposing projects that involve new and innovative elements, managers need to learn the importance of careful planning of both the substance and the story that is told to sell their idea. They must learn to listen to feedback that is critical both as a way to learn but also as a way to discover how arguments can be made more effective.

By way of example, let us consider the career of Jeff Immelt at GE. It is well documented and fascinating, although his strategy of growing GE through a focus on infrastructure development, water and clean energy, and health care delivery has attracted criticism from those who want the stable earnings growth provided by

Welch's financial services businesses. In addition, a badly handled earnings forecast has further irritated the critics. Nonetheless, Immelt remains the choice of GE's board.

Table 3-2 charts Jeff Immelt's career at GE. Certain features stand out. To begin, he spent an initial period being introduced to the company and trained in the sales function. He then spent five years in positions of increasing responsibility in the sales function of the Plastics group. A period of still greater responsibility followed in Home Appliances, followed by more assignments in Plastics and finally the top job in Medical Systems, a role in which Immelt distinguished himself by driving dramatic growth.

What is not apparent is the attention he received, from recruitment by one of GE's strong young line executives to an early presentation to GE's CEO, Jack Welch. The first assignment as a sales

TABLE 3-2

## Career time line for Jeff Immelt at General Electric Company

| | |
|---|---|
| 1982 | Enters GE on Commercial Leadership Program |
| 1983 | Manager—Business Development/GTX Product Management, GE Plastics |
| 1984 | Manager—Dallas District Sales, GE Plastics |
| 1986 | General Manager—Western Region Sales, GE Plastics |
| 1987 | General Manager—New Business Development & Marketing Development, GE Plastics |
| 1989 | Vice President of Consumer Service, GE Appliances |
| 1991 | Vice President of Worldwide Marketing and Product Management, GE Appliances |
| 1992 | Vice President Commercial Division, GE Plastics Americas |
| 1993 | Vice President and General Manager, GE Plastics Americas |
| 1997 | President and CEO, GE Medical Systems |
| November 2000 | President and Chairman-elect, GE; elected to board of directors |
| September 2001 | Chairman and CEO, General Electric Company |

*Source*: General Electric Company documents.

manager provided him with regular tough feedback on the importance of making the numbers, the foundation of accountability. Throughout his progress, he was mentored by the president of GE Plastics and tracked by the executive who recruited him, now a high-ranking member of GE's leadership team. Mentoring was complemented by annual feedback in GE's Session C, a robust process of detailed assessment and counseling. Having succeeded in driving growth in the Plastics business, Immelt next went to Home Appliances, a move chosen by Welch to provide Immelt with an ordeal by fire—the management of a huge product recall. Success with that problem was rewarded with promotion in Appliances. And progress there was followed by another stint in Plastics and then another promotion to a position in which inflation in raw material prices confronted Immelt with a brutal challenge to profitability. The resolution of that problem took time and involved weekly contact with Welch and the man who had recruited him, now GE's CFO. Immelt's eventual success led to the Medical Systems assignment, and a brilliant performance success.[20]

The case study from which this example is drawn makes clear that Immelt was tracked by the very top managers of GE and mentored on a regular basis from the moment he was recruited. Later, during trying periods, he received regular calls from Jack Welch tracking events and from GE's vice-chairman providing guidance. For inside-outsiders to flourish, mentoring is vital. The kind of personal detailed attention that Immelt received is key. No staff system can by itself cope with the idiosyncrasies of strong-minded folk as they learn to work in the context of teams and large organizations. They need to be called up short immediately when they have violated important norms and told how they can make amends so that the damage does not linger. They need to be protected from impatient elders, and their individuality nurtured and matured. That is how their ability to see the need for change is transformed from a nuisance into an asset. It is not easy, but when it happens, it is a delight.

Where the leadership of a company has supported the development of a cohort of inside-outsiders, the board's role is relatively simple to describe. Directors have to get to know the candidates, work with the CEO to frame criteria for choosing among them, and manage that process over its final months. Getting to know the candidates is a problem. Unless the board or its compensation committee has had independent access to the candidates, the board is really processing information provided by the CEO. Directors have heard about these people for years, but the information is provided by the company. To go beyond that, it is necessary to have a program of visits, and the CEO has to agree to stay out of the way. That is a very unusual set of arrangements.

The second challenge is to reach consensus in the board as to the nature of the strategic challenges facing the company over the next five to ten years and *the implication of that judgment* for the choice of a leader. Interestingly, this may be a very different discussion from the one the board has been having with the incumbent CEO. The new ingredient is extreme focus on those aspects of the world ahead that will require new capabilities from the company and hence new attributes for the leader. This is an aspect of the process in which the board may have an advantage. If its members have knowledge relevant to the business, their judgments may well complement those of senior management. Other issues of importance in this circumstance involve attempts to retain the "losers" in the company if that is the desire of the board, the structuring of new assignments of top officers during the transition, and determining the role of the departing CEO.

## Incumbent to Outsider

For an outsider, the transition to leadership is a brutal learning process in which *industry knowledge, organizational knowledge,* and *leadership skills appropriate to the culture* are engaged with the challenges of the company. It is certainly possible that the first and third criteria can be met by an outsider, although it is easy to misunderstand important subtle differences between industries. A great marketer of branded power tools from Black & Decker can have a hard time with nonbranded housewares. This was the problem when Joseph Galli moved from Black & Decker to Newell. Similarly, leadership skills that worked well in one culture may be quite inappropriate to another. That would appear to be the problem when Juergen Schremp's team from Daimler moved to Chrysler.[21] Organizational knowledge is a huge barrier to the outsider that can only be overcome with time and early success.

Lack of any of the three forms of knowledge and skills raises the probability of failure. The fact that knowledge of industry, organization, and culture is company-specific makes taking over especially daunting for an outsider.[22] The importance of these factors certainly suggests the lines of questioning that the search committee of the board should follow. But if board members are not deeply familiar with the industry, organization, and culture—not improbable when looking for an outsider—they may be in a poor position to make the necessary judgments.

Unless the board has found a new leader that meets the three criteria, the best it will get is a period of improved earnings. But it will be a miracle if major strategic issues that influence longer-term growth will be faced and resolved. It does happen—Lou Gerstner kept IBM integrated; Charlotte Beers restored the advertising agency Ogilvy & Mather's client base and renewed the firm's culture. But it is far more typical for the new CEO to leave after a few years—or sell the company. The 2007 study of CEO succession by Booz Allen Hamilton reports that "outsiders tend to have shorter tenures than insiders. For outgoing CEOs in 2007, the mean outsider tenure was 4.8 years, compared to 6.4 years for insiders."[23]

## The Role of the Board of Directors in CEO Succession

The foregoing arguments make for a dismal recitation. How can a board help avoid a negative succession outcome? The first step is to understand how much work has to be done by the CEO and his or her top team, how early they have to start, and how extensively all key aspects of the way the company is run must be involved to support leadership development. Succession is not an event. Most of this chapter has described a *process* by which over the years talent is recruited to the company and developed, a pool of high-potential candidates is identified, assignments are chosen to develop those candidate's talents further, and opportunities are provided to prove their mettle. Only management can do that work—not the board.

The next step is to help the CEO focus on that challenge. It isn't easy. If a company does not have a tradition of building talent, and if it is not organized so that talent can develop without turning the process into a wrestling contest, it takes time to build the human resources organization—starting with a first-class chief talent officer. It may take time just to persuade the CEO that this is a marvelous opportunity, not a threat, which may be difficult for an insecure CEO, or an imperial CEO, or a CEO preoccupied with poor current performance.

If the succession question and a clear program of leadership development are not on the table five years before the incumbent CEO might leave, then there is an issue. A CEO who provides thoughtful leadership of the process for the board will pick an early time to initiate discussion of the topic or respond with alacrity when it is first raised by the board. The head of HR will be trusted and capable of staffing the process. In the opposite case, if the CEO is reluctant, the lead board director or functional equivalent has to force the issue. In other words, the job of the board is to get the CEO to do the job. The board cannot do the job itself.

The next step is to establish a process in which a pool of CEO candidates is identified and developed. Identifying the pool is very important. The pool should be as large as possible. The mavericks who might be inside-outsiders need to be on the list. Who built a new business? Who led the exit from a core business? Who has transformed the core so that what was once in decline is now a platform for future growth? These are the kind of achievements one should be seeking.

The subsequent steps are more obvious. The pool is pruned, the candidates are selected, a final choice made, and the transition managed. The board needs to spend time on each of these steps. It should be the preoccupation of the governance and nominating committee. In particular, the board or the committee should meet the candidates and get to know their strengths and weaknesses.

The process need not be a horse race among candidates. Although a leader must be chosen, the entire team is an asset. One company I recently studied was able to keep a cohort of five leading next-generation executives, promoting all to take over the company working for a collectively chosen leader. I had never before seen this trick accomplished, but it suggests that a great deal can be achieved when the CEO and board start early and work together. When a board is passive, none of this may happen. Reassurance that "we have several good candidates" or "I have a 'name in the envelope' that I have discussed with the lead director" are no substitute for careful extended discussions as part of the succession process outlined earlier. When the board intrudes and tries to manage the process directly, its interference with the operations of the company can lead to a crisis of governance. The board can insist that there be a succession development process. But because the process is a central aspect of the way the company is managed, it cannot be carried out by the board.

The board can—indeed must—inquire regularly about the process, track the progress of candidates, and meet as many as possible—but it cannot do the recruiting and talent development required. It cannot get into the details of organizational arrangements that ensure that talented executives have the opportunity to experience general management responsibility early in their careers. Most important, it cannot be present during the critical times when plans and budgets are developed and outcomes reviewed that turn out to be the most critical "teaching moments" for mentors.

As long as the steps in the succession process are accomplished, there is no formula for how management and the board accomplish their task. Once again, the keys are early attention to recruiting and developing talent; a large pool of candidates; further development that favors inside-outsiders where they can be found; careful pruning and then selection against future-oriented criteria; a period of transition that gives the new CEO a maximum chance to succeed;

and, finally, extensive exposure to those on the board who will make the final choice at every step of the way.

If a board can check off each of these steps, the chances are very good that the next CEO will succeed.

# Notes

1. See, for example, J. W. Lorsch and R. C. Clark, "Leading from the Boardroom," *Harvard Business Review*, April 2008, 104–111.

2. The entire argument is laid out in depth in my book summarizing that research, *The CEO Within: Why Inside Outsiders Are Key to Succession Planning* (Boston: Harvard Business School Press, 2007).

3. William Fruhan, unpublished memorandum, October 1, 2007, Exhibit C. See also R. Foster and S. Kaplan, *Creative Destruction* (New York: Doubleday, 2001), 47.

4. See, for example, Y. Doz and M. Kosonen, *Fast Strategy: How Strategic Agility Will Help You Stay Ahead of the Game* (Harlow, England: Pearson/Longman, 2008).

5. Robert H. Hayes, Steven C. Wheelwright, and Kim B. Clark, *Dynamic Manufacturing: Creating the Learning Organization* (New York: The Free Press, 1988), 340–348; and Clayton M. Christensen and Michael E. Raynor, *The Innovator's Solution: Creating and Sustaining Successful Growth* (Boston: Harvard Business School Publishing Corporation, 2003), 267–284.

6. J. Collins, *Good to Great* (New York: Collins Business, 2001).

7. B. Groysberg, A. N. McLean, and N. Nohria, "Are Leaders Portable?" *Harvard Business Review*, May 2006; and Bower, *The CEO Within.*

8. P.-O. Karlsson, G. L. Neilson, and J. C. Webster, "CEO Succession 2007: The Performance Paradox," *Strategy + Business*, no. 51 (Summer 2008).

9. Kenneth Andrews, *The Concept of Corporate Strategy*, revised edition (Burr Ridge, IL: Richard D. Irwin, 1980), 5–12.

10. See, for example, David Garvin, "Emerging Business Opportunities at IBM (A)," Case 304075 (Boston: Harvard Business School, 2004); and A. M. Kleinbaum, T. E. Stuart, and M. Tushman, "Communication (and Coordination) in the Modern Corporation," working paper, 2008.

11. Doz and Kosonen, *Fast Strategy: How Strategic Agility Will Help You Stay Ahead of the Game* (London: Pearson Education Ltd., 2008), 9.

12. Bower, *The CEO Within*, 13.

13. Society of Human Resource Management, "SHRM Weekly Online Poll," December 2003, results reported in S. Meisinger, "The King Is Dead, Long Live the King!" *HR Magazine* 49, no. 6 (2004).

14. J. L. Bower and S. E. Hout, "GE: The People Factory at Work," video, product number 8107 (Boston: Harvard Business School, 2002).

15. Bower, *The CEO Within*, 211–212.

16. Karlsson, Neilson, and Webster, "CEO Succession 2007."

17. R. Khurana, *Searching for a Corporate Savior: The Irrational Quest for Charismatic CEOs* (Princeton, NJ: Princeton University Press, 2002).

18. Ibid.

19. C. Lucier, S. Wheeler, and R. Habbel, "CEO Succession 2006: The Era of the Inclusive Leader," *Strategy + Business,* no. 47 (Summer 2007).

20. C. A. Bartlett and A. N. McLean, "The GE Talent Machine: The Making of a CEO," Case 304–049 (Boston: Harvard Business School, rev. November 3, 2006).

21. B. Vlasic and B. A. Stertz, *Taken for a Ride: How Daimler-Benz Drove Off with Chrysler* (New York: William Morrow, 2000), for example, 318–321.

22. As an aside, the high risks associated with an outsider as CEO have a good deal to do with the issue of high CEO compensation. Because most outside candidates are employed and successful at the time they are recruited, they must be paid a premium to leave a lower-risk situation. These high-compensation packages then become part of the industry averages that compensation consultants use to counsel companies considering the pay of insiders. Despite its reservations, it is easy to see why a board that values its CEO highly would consider it unfair to pay him or her less than some new arrival to the industry with nothing but a resume. As economists tell us, the price at the margin establishes the market.

23. Karlsson, Neilson, and Webster, "CEO Succession 2007."

*Four*

# The Pay Problem

*Time for a New Paradigm for*
*Executive Compensation*

JAY W. LORSCH

AND RAKESH KHURANA

Concerns about the compensation of chief executive officers and other top executives of American public companies have reached fever pitch since the financial crisis and the economic meltdown of 2009. Some observers blame the recent recession in part on the flawed compensation arrangements for the top management of major financial institutions. Such concerns are not new. For almost twenty years, a growing chorus of voices—including some shareholders, the business media, policy makers, and academics—have been criticizing the way top managers are paid. The criticisms focus particularly on CEOs not only because they are the highest paid, but also because their compensation sets the pattern for executives beneath them.

Previously published in *Harvard Magazine*, May–June 2010, 30–35.

Like previous criticisms, the current complaints focus on two issues: executives are paid too much, and current incentive-pay schemes are flawed because the connection between executive pay and company performance is mixed at best—and at worst has led to a series of dysfunctional behaviors.

Whether executives are paid too much is highly contested. Some institutional shareholders, politicians, and the public (as measured by opinion surveys) believe that CEOs are overpaid, while other shareholders, board members, and executives themselves disagree. What cannot be disputed is that American CEOs make more money than CEOs in other countries, largely because of a greater reliance on incentive pay (figure 4-1). Further, American CEOs are paid increasingly large amounts relative to the average employee

FIGURE 4-1

## CEO total compensation controlling for sales and industry

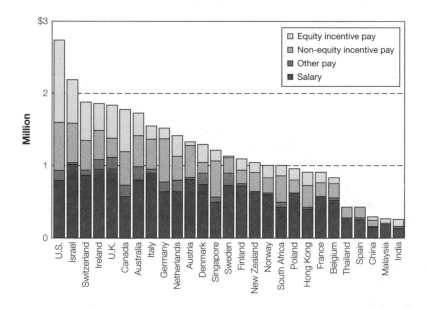

Note: This figure compares CEO pay in U.S. dollars in each country, controlling for firm size (sales) and industry. The sample fiscal year is 2006. For each country, the study estimates the US$ pay for a CEO running a hypothetical firm with $1 billion sales using the estimated coefficient for pay-size sensitivity and that country's dummy variable, controlling for "average" industry. Countries are sorted in descending order in terms of total estimated pay.

Source: Nuno Fernandes, Miguel A. Ferreira, Pedro Matos, and Kevin J. Murphy, "The Pay Divide: Why Are (U.S.) Top Executives Paid More?" ECGI Working Paper Series in Finance, August 2009, 41.

(table 4-1) and their immediate subordinates (figure 4-2). Finally, it is clear that the rise in executive pay contributes to the skewing of income distribution in the United States (figure 4-3).

Less clear is evidence about the link between executive compensation and performance. The most comprehensive survey examining the link between CEO pay and performance found that changes in firm performance account for only 4 percent of the variance in CEO pay.[1] This may in part reflect CEOs' ability to game the system, or even the perverse effects of incentives that promote *dysfunctional* behavior.

The solutions offered for the problems of excessive levels of executive pay and the need to strengthen the link between pay and performance often hit on the same themes: strengthen the

TABLE 4-1

## Ratio of average CEO pay to average worker pay

|  | 1980 | 1990 | 2005 | 2006 | 2007 |
|---|---|---|---|---|---|
| Ratio of average CEO pay to average worker pay | 44:1 | 107:1 | 411:1 | 364:1 | 344:1 |

*Sources*: 2008, 2007, and 2006 Executive Excess Reports, Institute for Policy Studies and United for a Fair Economy, http://faireconomy.org/executive_oxcess_reports.

FIGURE 4-2

## Median total compensation for top 500 firms

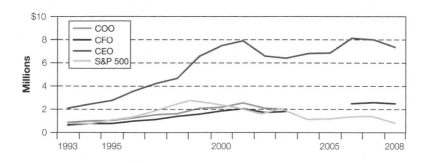

*Note*: The figure shows 2008 median total compensation data comprising roughly one hundred data from those companies that had filed by June 2009.

*Source*: V.G. Narayanan, "Nature of Compensation Plans" (paper presented at the Harvard Business School conference on executive compensation, September 2009). Data from Standard & Poor's Execucomp Database.

FIGURE 4-3

## Household income dispersion, 1980–2008

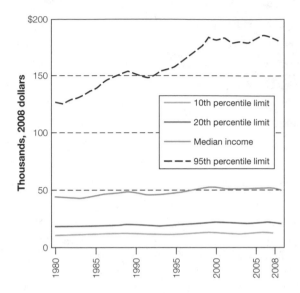

Legend:
- 10th percentile limit
- 20th percentile limit
- Median income
- 95th percentile limit

*Source*: U.S Census Bureau, Historical Income Inequality Tables, Table A-3: Selected Measures of Household Income Dispersion: 1967 to 2008, http://www.census.gov/hhes/www/income/histinc/IE-1.pdf.

independence of directors and compensation committees; increase the shareholders' rights to elect directors and to express their views on compensation plans, to discourage gaming and align incentives more closely with the aims of the owners. It is also tempting to suggest that these problems can be solved by better compensation schemes or improved techniques to link CEO pay to stock performance.

We disagree with the premises underlying these remedies. Instead, we find that the current compensation trouble stems in large part from unexamined assumptions that have fundamentally changed the nature of executive compensation and radically shifted the way that boards, executives, and even the larger society regard the corporation and its broader purpose.

In fact, the problems of executive compensation are symptomatic of larger societal questions. They cannot be resolved without considering the purpose of executive compensation—what behaviors, attitudes, and values we are trying to motivate in our business leaders—and indeed the larger purpose of business in American society. We assert that the current approach to executive compensation is an outgrowth of a pervasive paradigm that boards, senior executives, and indeed even those of us educating future and current business leaders have adopted about the purpose of the corporation, what it means to be a business executive, and to whom and for what executives are responsible.

## The American Way of Pay

To understand our perspective requires understanding how corporate America arrived at its current compensation policies. In mid-twentieth-century business articles and textbooks, one finds references to executive "salaries"; mention of incentives (in cash, stock, or options) is an exception. As a management professor stated in 1951, "It is usually unwise to have a large proportion of executive pay consist of incentives."[2]

### Complexity and Consultants

By the 1970s and 1980s, however, compensation packages for CEOs and other senior executives included more incentives, and those incentives were paid in stock and options as well as cash. These arrangements were often worked out in discussions and negotiations between the CEO and the compensation committee of the board of directors, and then ratified by the entire board. As the complexity of companies and their compensation arrangements increased, a new actor emerged to provide ideas and advice to both executives and corporate directors—the compensation consultant. Because these consultants promoted themselves as disinterested, objective experts, many board members with limited time and knowledge about compensation matters came, not surprisingly, to depend on—and increasingly accept, uncritically—the consultants' advice.

At the core of that advice was the alleged power of incentive compensation to motivate executives. Directors often found themselves sympathetic to such an idea, and perhaps also were compromised about the basic premises behind CEO pay by the fact that they were often active CEOs themselves. But the advice about the importance and efficacy of such incentives was based more on the power of an idea than on clear empirical data. Moreover, the consultants had their own reasons to keep their client executives happy. As Arch Paton, a McKinsey partner and compensation expert, explained in 1985, "For their part the consultants like to satisfy this well meaning desire of the executive and frequently have substantial other income from the client to protect. This could create a conflict of interest[,] for consultant recommendations below the expectations of the executive might not be well received. Further[,] as time goes on[,] the consultant may come to regard the *executive* as his client rather than the *company*."[3] [Emphasis added.]

### The Motivation Model

The underlying assumption—that executives would work more effectively if their monetary rewards were tied to the results they were achieving—built on earlier ideas about incentives for factory workers, sales representatives, and so on, that go back to the piece-rate schemes advocated by Frederick Taylor and other proponents of scientific management. But these prescriptions missed two complications when applied to senior executives:

- Very often executives have little or no control over the results they are supposedly being rewarded for achieving.

- The results of a company are more often produced by a group of executives or even by an entire organization's effort, and only rarely by a single individual. Although some scholars had pointed out that incentives work only when individuals had a clear "line of sight" between their efforts, the results achieved, and the rewards being offered, such complications were increasingly ignored as boards accepted the consultants' assumption about what motivated executives.[4]

A related and equally unexamined assumption was that executives worked primarily for money. Such rewards as future promotions, the intrinsic satisfaction of achieving results, and the pride taken in belonging to a successful company were overlooked and sometimes denigrated. Even for American business executives who value the "almighty dollar" so highly, these other rewards have important meaning. That is another reason for our strong reservations about whether the heavy reliance on incentive compensation delivers the results that its proponents believe it does.

## The Market Fallacy

Even as attitudes toward executive compensation changed inside firms, changes related to the larger market for CEOs—and a new intellectual framework about the purpose of the corporation— would complete the superstructure that has governed the executive compensation process for more than three decades.

Increasing turnover in chief executive suites contributed to a belief that there is a robust and well-functioning market for senior executive talent against which compensation needs to be benchmarked. By "robust and well-functioning," we mean a market in which many buyers and sellers make transactions anonymously. In such a market, what and how an executive should be paid is defined by the supply and demand for the talent he or she represents. Though there can be little doubt that such a market exists for middle-level executives, there are fewer "buyers" and "sellers" when one considers senior-level executives, and the transaction is not transparent until much later, if at all. Therefore market rates are much harder to identify, and the compensation arrangements in reality depend much more on negotiations between the executive (and usually his or her attorney) and the compensation committee and its advisers. For senior executives, the most significant determinants of compensation are the negotiating skill and bargaining power of the parties involved. These negotiations cover not only the amounts to be paid but also the form of the compensation, as well as the performance metrics, if any, to which it is to be related.

This flawed assumption about the "market" for CEO talent flows from two factors that have driven up senior executive compensation. First, given the idea that there is such a market, compensation consultants have sought a method for making market rates transparent—the much-discussed compensation surveys that establish the "price" of various executive positions by company size, industry, and geography. Not only is the validity of such a methodology questionable, but also the surveys have the perverse effect of "ratcheting" compensation ever upward (to use Warren Buffett's term).

It works like this: The surveys report compensation for a position by quartiles—from highest to lowest amounts. Not surprisingly, compensation committees and their fellow directors prefer the upper quartile. It not only makes the executives feel better, but it looks better in the company's Compensation Discussion and Analysis (CD&A) in its annual 10-K report to the Securities and Exchange Commission (SEC). If the executives don't want the public to be told they are below average in pay (and presumably performance), neither do many directors and shareholders. That would imply that the board of the company (in which shareholders have invested) believe its performance is below average. As a result, American senior executives are like the children of Lake Wobegon—all above average. Recent papers suggest further that executives game the system of comparisons, making the benchmark against which they are being judged a moving target that is too often manipulated by the directors, compensation consultants, and even the executives themselves.[5,6] If the executive's performance falls short of the original target, it is too often the target that is reset, often surreptitiously in the company's financial footnotes.[7,8]

Although compensation committees and their advisers act in the belief that they are dealing with a *market,* they actually find themselves involved in *negotiations.* In numerous papers and books, Jessie Friedman and Lucian Bebchuk have argued that when directors negotiate with an executive, their proposals are constrained not only by their beliefs about market conditions, but also by their bargaining power and tactics. Nowhere is this clearer than in the case of the large lump-sum payments commonly granted to executives, especially when they are brought in from outside the company. These are typically of two types: "make whole" payments (money given to an executive to replace earnings that he or she will leave behind with the former employer) and "golden parachutes" (money guaranteed to the executive if the company is acquired by or merged into another firm). Both payments are guaranteed regardless of the executive's performance, unless he or she should be fired for cause (which, according to the etiquette of corporate America, never happens). Such payments, because of their large size and lack of a link to performance, are another important cause of the rise in top-level compensation—and are a major source of shareholder concern.

Yet compensation committees continue to grant these lump sums to new executives, because that is what they believe the market requires to attract the new talent. The idea of bargaining about the size of such payments, or about making them contingent on performance, seems to be off the table.

The behavior of General Electric's board as it was beginning the process of selecting a successor to the retiring Jack Welch illustrates the elevator effect on pay. Five possible candidates were identified about two years in advance of Welch's departure. He suggested to the compensation committee and the board that each executive be granted a multimillion-dollar retention bonus to encourage him to stay at GE and compete for the top spot. When directors expressed concern about the cost to GE shareholders of all these bonuses, they were told that they would have to pay only the person who was selected as Welch's successor: the others were all likely to leave GE to be CEOs elsewhere, and their new employers would pay the promised amount as a "make whole arrangement."[9]

### "Agents" and Owners: The Primacy of Stock

The second factor that transformed compensation was the theory that linked top executives' pay plans to a firm's stock price.[10] Taking as a starting point the earlier work of Adolph Berle and Gardiner Means, economists Michael Jensen, William Meckling, and others argued that corporate directors and senior executives were "agents" of the company's shareholders.[11] It followed that the goal of boards and the executives whose compensation they set must be to align these agents' interests with the owners', most directly by maximizing shareholder wealth. Thus executive incentives should be tied to "shareholder value," usually measured by the company's stock price and dividends per share.

Few ideas about business have been as quickly and widely embraced not only by directors and executives, but also by the bankers, consultants, and lawyers who advise them, as well as by the Delaware Court of Chancery. Prominent business organizations switched from advocating a "stakeholder view" in corporate decision making to embracing the "shareholder" maximization imperative. In 1990, for instance, the Business Roundtable, a group of CEOs of the largest U.S. companies, still emphasized in its mission statement that "the directors' responsibility is to carefully weigh the interests of all stakeholders as part of their responsibility to the corporation or to the long-term interests of its shareholders." By 1997, the same organization argued that "the paramount duty of management and of boards of directors is to the corporation's stockholders; the interests of other stakeholders are relevant as a derivative of the duty to the stockholders."

In applying these ideas to executive compensation plans, consultants, directors, and the executives themselves had a problem. In most instances, the executives had only partial control over the factors that determined the value of their company's stock. A company's past or likely future performance was only one determinant of the current share price; the general stock market level and broader economic conditions also affected shareholder value significantly. The most widely accepted solution to this complication was to tie executive compensation to economic goals seen as drivers of shareholder value (return on assets, return on equity, growth in sales or profits or both, etc.), while paying the executives in stock or in options: a purportedly perfect alignment of interests and incentives.

## The Compensation System

Taken together, these assumptions—which are still widely shared by directors, executives, and those who advise them—have created (with a little help from the IRS)[12] a near-universal set of beliefs about the components of effective compensation for senior executives (table 4-2), as a glance at the CD&A section in the 10-K of any public company will show. Those components include a base salary

TABLE 4-2

## Typical compensation plan

| Salary | Annual incentive | Long-term incentive plan | Lump-sum payments | Retirement benefits |
|---|---|---|---|---|
| Fixed income | Performance based | Performance based | Unrelated to performance | Unrelated to performance |
| • Except for the top 350 firms, usually a maximum of $1 million. But, even for these larger firms, salary is capped because of the IRS code. | • Paid in cash and/or stock<br><br>• Usually paid as a percentage of base salary<br><br>• Based on individual and/or company annual performance measures (financial, strategic, and/or operational) | • Paid in stock and/or stock options<br><br>• A reward for long-term performance (usually defined as 3 years)<br><br>• Typical options vest based on the efflux of time (3–6 years)<br><br>• Performance-based option grants vest based on EPS or stock performance | • Make-whole, golden parachutes, and change of control payments, as well as other contractually obligated payments | • Defined benefit plans and/or deferred compensation plans<br><br>• Use of company aircraft and cars<br><br>• Consulting arrangements |

*Source*: J. Slivanya and K. Powers, "IRS Increases Scrutiny of Performance-Based Plans Under Sec. 162(m)," *The Tax Adviser*, September 1, 2008, 561–562, http://www.proquest.com.ezp-prod1.hul.harvard.edu/.

(usually $1 million). There is also a bonus related to annual company performance (usually paid in cash and stock), and a long-term incentive based on three years of company performance, even though in many industries (such as pharmaceuticals) a three-year time frame can hardly be considered "long term." Most plans also include the make-whole payments and golden parachutes described earlier.

This unanimity should not be surprising, because a handful of consultants who share these assumptions advise the boards of all major American companies. The validity of "agency" theory has been widely accepted and provides the intellectual underpinnings for many aspects of these plans, even though many of its original advocates have recognized its limits and imperfections.[13]

## The Causes—and Consequences—of Rising Executive Pay

The major causes of the escalating pay for CEOs and other senior executives flow from these assumptions. The most obvious connection is the ratcheting effect of the compensation surveys. Less obvious, but also significant, is the fact that until the downturn in 2008, the economic performance of publicly traded companies had been on an upward trend for a decade or longer. Even though we have doubts that their incentive plans actually motivated managers to act to cause their companies to perform better, if company results improved for *any* reason (including pure serendipity), the managers received higher pay: cause and effect didn't matter. What drove incentive compensation up was the company's performance itself— whether under the control of the CEO and his or her team or not.

During this same period, the value of shares of U.S. companies was also rising. Because the largest proportion of senior executive compensation is in company stock, as the value of the company's shares rose, so did the amount of pay the executives received. Finally, wide adoption of lump-sum payments increased compensation still further.

What most troubles us is that executive pay is rising not so much as a *driver* of improved performance but as a *consequence* of improving performance and an accompanying rise in equity values. And as we explained earlier, incentives have an impact on behavior only when the recipients can see a direct link from their actions to the results achieved and the rewards they will receive. As we have argued, in most companies *multiple* forces and the joint efforts of *many* individuals cause the results achieved. There are circumstances when executives can see an opportunity—a direct connection between actions they can take and results that will produce rewards they desire—but not in the way their companies intend: for example, decisions to cut corners on approving mortgages to earn greater origination fees (and the resulting waves of loan losses and foreclosures), or the decisions taken at Enron to create off-balance-sheet transactions (disguising that failed corporation's true, deteriorating results). In these circumstances, the potential payouts worked *too* well, causing executives to take unwise or even illegal actions.

As a society, we understand how to deal with specific transgressions like these by making them difficult or legally risky to carry out. But when the transgressions arise because fallacious assumptions become accepted practices among our business and professional leaders, we seem to have no effective antidotes. The SEC can require greater disclosure about top management compensation in the CD&A—but the likely result is executives comparing their pay with each other to make sure they are being fairly treated. Or Congress can change the tax code (as it did in 1993) so that salaries above $1 million would be taxed at an excess rate—but the dubious effect was to put *more* emphasis on incentive compensation, accompanied by all the problems just described.

Congress has called for "say on pay" (a measure adopted in the United Kingdom), thus giving shareholders the right to hold a nonbinding vote on top executives' compensation—but shareholders are likely to be trapped in the same misleading assumptions as boards have been. We need to rethink *how* we pay senior executives, and *for what*, so that they are motivated not only to create wealth for themselves but also to build companies that serve society.

## Revising the American Compensation Paradigm

The issue of CEO compensation goes beyond absolute amounts and the technical terms defining how executives are paid. Indeed, we believe that the existing approach to compensation offers a poignant commentary on the kind of society we are becoming. Compensation systems always become in part *ends*, not simply *means*. By emphasizing particular ends, reward systems condition the behavior and thinking of those people who participate in them or feel their effects. Over time, they shape the business paradigm. In turn, because business is such a central institution in American society, they also shape our national culture and character.[14] The contemporary pay system is an important part of a radical shift in what we in America regard as the essential nature of corporations, their purpose, and the role and identity of business leaders.

For most of the twentieth century, the large, public corporation was regarded as both an *economic* entity and a *social* institution. Shareholders were but one of several constituencies that stood in relation to the corporation.[15] Corporate decisions were evaluated not only by their specific economic results but also with an eye toward their moral and political consequences.[16]

Today, corporations are typically described in terms of economic and financial considerations alone. Within this dominant paradigm, corporations are seen simply as groups of self-interested market actors—shareholders, employees, executives, or customers—held together by nothing more than a series of contracts.[17] These supposedly voluntary contracts define the transactions between executive and employee, for example, in a mutually advantageous way.[18] Once the contractually defined exchange is completed, the parties to such a relationship have no further obligations toward each other: they revert to the status of anonymous market actors.

This image of the corporation is problematic, however: it has nothing to say about the unavoidable fact that organizations are themselves complex social systems.[19] Organizational relationships are not merely transactional and fleeting. Over time, they become imbued with affect, content, norms, values, culture, and meaning. Defining the organization as a nexus of individual contracts conveniently dispenses with issues of power, coercion, and exploitation.[20] It denies *any* unique relationship between an organization and other constituents. In all these ways, and more, this model is at odds with more than a century's research in psychology, sociology, anthropology, and organizational behavior on actual workplace relations. Without empirical justification, it relieves the corporate institution of any meaningful responsibility to anyone but the transitory group of stockholders who buy and sell shares constantly.[21]

We need to change the terms of the conversation, to make room for a larger and more public discussion about the purpose of the corporation and larger moral and political considerations. Every corporation is embedded in a social matrix and is accountable for multiple factors within that social setting: obligations to the society that provides it tax advantages or public goods, such as public schooling, publicly financed research, or basic infrastructure such as roads and airports.[22] In a democratic society like the United States, the general public expects responsible and ethical practices and the exercise of self-restraint among business leaders in exchange for vesting an extraordinary amount of power that affects society's well-being in private, corporate hands.[23] Indeed, the primary problem in this perspective is the agency problem we described earlier, in which all the actors are trying to protect themselves from the self-interested actions of everyone else.[24]

As part of that broader public conversation, we also need to revisit what has happened to the identity of management and what it means to be a manager. In part, we believe that the perspective and practices that now undergird executive compensation have themselves mutated the identity of managers fundamentally. At places like Harvard Business School, the prevailing paradigm regards managers as relentless, self-interested free agents ready to make tracks out of their companies and to sacrifice the long term for immediate gain. That view has largely displaced earlier views of managers as professionals with obligations to various "stakeholders" and to the broader society.[25] The dominant ethos today also legitimates the notion that human beings are relentless market maximizers who need literally to be *bribed* to focus solely on shareholder value—undermining other commitments managers might have to employees, customers, the community, or larger national and global concerns such as the environment or human rights.

Both of us have dedicated our professional lives to business education; we believe deeply in the power of profit-driven business as an institution. But business is useful only if it serves as a means toward an end. We are now presented with choices about sustainability, pandemics, economic and social justice, and the environment that concern nothing less than our collective destiny. The technical forces in play, the global interrelations, the destructive effects on the real economy of badly managed and largely speculative financial dealings, the unrestrained exploitation of our planet's nonrenewable resources—all of this should lead us to reflect on the type of capitalist *system* we have created and the types of *people* who are leading it.[26]

The recent economic crisis and the role that our compensation systems played in fomenting it require a holistic reexamination not only of compensation but of the assumptions and values underlying the economic system we have created. Our present condition offers us a unique opportunity to reenvision our journey and our ultimate destination. Rethinking the nature of executive pay within the context of our larger economic and social system and the challenges we face may enable us to create a new model of compensation rooted in a more realistic recognition of the social context within which firms operate. It should, and can, rest on valid assumptions and fundamental values that allow us to build a more inclusive and sustainable economic future—one in which we don't have to bribe executives to do the duties we have entrusted to them.

## A First Step

A rethinking of the manner in which CEOs and other senior executives are compensated can be a powerful signal to those executives and the wider society that corporate America recognizes the importance of this broader view of the role of business in American society. The power to achieve these innovations is currently in the hands of every board of directors and especially their compensation committees. All that is required is for them to recognize the importance of the new assumptions that we have emphasized earlier.

First, recognize that incentives only have motivational power if they reward outcomes over which the executives have control. This means providing rewards for company economic outcomes, which top managers can affect, and not for the gyrations in the stock market, over which corporate leaders have less control. This approach will ensure that incentive plans achieve a "line of sight" between the efforts of the executives, the results they achieve, and the rewards they are paid. This will provide the greatest likelihood that the incentives are truly motivating these leaders. It also sends a clear message to all connected to the company that the ultimate purpose of its board and management is to focus on achieving corporate health. This also raises the matter of the time frame for these rewards. If the name of the game is corporate health, how far into the future should the efforts be focused? Although the answer obviously varies from one industry to another, clearly the time horizon at a minimum should be several years.

Because long-term corporate results depend on the collaborative efforts of a group of senior executives, compensation plans should significantly reward such group behavior. Although executives can be paid for individual achievement, they also should be rewarded for their collaborative effort.

It is also important to recognize that monetary rewards (either in shares or cash) are only one type of the rewards that have meaning for senior executives. Feedback in performance reviews and promotion to more responsible positions are among other factors that these executives obviously see as rewarding. Therefore, monetary rewards and these other rewards should be aligned for the most motivational impact.

The approach we are describing is obviously intended to tie compensation to corporate long-term performance. We are not suggesting that annual incentive plans should be eliminated—only that they be designed to also contribute to longer-term performance beyond just the current year. We do believe, however, that the approach we are arguing for should eliminate all lump-sum payments not tied to performance (e.g., golden parachutes, make-whole payments). If the new executive is coming in from outside the company, any such payments must still be conditional on achieving performance targets. More broadly, as we suggested earlier, the compensation committee must recognize that its job in creating compensation plans for "outside" executives is a matter of negotiation, and they need to be prepared for this process.

# Notes

1. H. L. Tosi, S. Werner, J. P. Katz, and L. R. Gomez-Mejia, "How Much Does Performance Matter? A Meta-Analysis of CEO Pay Studies," *Journal of Management* 26 (2000): 301–340.

2. William H. Newman, *Administrative Action: The Techniques of Organization and Management* (New York: Prentice-Hall, 1950), 365.

3. Arch Patton, "Those Million-Dollar-A-Year Executives," *Harvard Business Review,* January–February 1985, 56–62.

4. Edward E. Lawler, *Pay and Organizational Effectiveness: A Psychological View* (New York: McGraw-Hill, 1971).

5. Thomas A. DiPrete, Greg Eirich, and Matthew Pittinksy, "Compensation Benchmarking, Leapfrogs, and the Surge in Executive Pay," *American Journal of Sociology* 115 (2010): 1671–1712.

6. Adair Morse, Vikram Nanda, and Amit Seru, "Are Incentive Contracts Rigged by Powerful CEOs?" AFA 2006 Boston meetings paper; EFA 2006 Zurich meetings paper, November 2008, http://ssrn.com/abstract=687504.

7. Rakesh Khurana and James Weber, "AFL-CIO: Office of Investment and Home Depot," Case 407-907 (Boston: Harvard Business School, 2007).

8. Charles A. O'Reilly III and Brian G. M. Main, "Economic and Psychological Perspectives on CEO Compensation: A Review and Synthesis," *Industrial and Corporate Change* 19 (June 2010): 675–712.

9. Personal correspondence.

10. Michael C. Jensen and William H. Meckling, "Theory of the Firm: Managerial Behavior, Agency Costs and Ownership Structure," *Journal of Financial Economics* 3 (1976): 303–360.

11. Adolph Berle and Gardiner Means, *The Modern Corporation and Private Property* (New York: Macmillan, 1933).

12. In 1993, the IRS issued Section 162(m), which dictates that non-performance-based compensation in excess of $1 million is not tax deductible. This applies to the CEO and the three other most highly paid executives reported in SEC filings.

13. Michael Jensen, Kevin Murphy, and Eric Wruck, "Remuneration: Where We've Been, How We Got to Here, What Are the Problems, and How to Fix

Them," Harvard NOM working paper no. 04-28; ECGI– Finance working paper no. 44/2004, July 2004, http://ssrn.com/abstract=561305.

14. For thoughtful accounts on the link between the economic system and social values, see Tony Judt, *Ill Fares the Land* (New York: Penguin Press, 2010) and Robert N. Bellah et al., *Habits of the Heart: Individualism and Commitment in America* (New York: Harper & Row, 1985).

15. Edward Freeman, "The Politics of Stakeholder Theory: Some Future Directions," *Business Ethics Quarterly* 4, no. 4 (1994): 409–422.

16. F. Dobbin and D. Zorn, "Corporate Malfeasance and the Myth of Shareholder Value," *Political Power and Social Theory* 17 (2005): 179–198.

17. For an excellent description of how this financialization model has shaped the culture in Wall Street investment firms, see Karen Ho, *Liquidated: An Ethnography of Wall Street* (Durham, NC: Duke University Press, 2009).

18. The best recent description of the societal implications of this idea is in Thomas Ehrlich, Anne Colby, and William Sullivan, "Business Education and the Liberal Arts," working paper, Carnegie Foundation for the Advancement of Teaching. We are indebted to their discussions of the implications of agency theory for managerial identity.

19. P. J. DiMaggio and W. Powell, "The Iron Cage Revisited: Institutional Isomorphism and Collective Rationality in Organizational Fields," *American Sociological Review* 48, no. 2 (1983): 147–160.

20. C. Perrow, *Complex Organizations: A Critical Essay*, 2nd ed. (New York: Random House, 1979).

21. Ibid.

22. Judt, *Ill Fares the Land*.

23. Anne Colby, Thomas Ehrlich, Elizabeth Beaumont, and Jason Stephens, *Educating Citizens* (San Francisco: Jossey Bass, 2003). See also William M. Sullivan, *Reconstructing Public Philosophy* (Berkeley: University of California Press, 1986).

24. One excellent example of how theoretical constructs end up shaping human behavior is Sumantra Ghoshal, "Bad Management Theories Are Destroying Good Management Practices," *Academy of Management Learning and Education* 4, no. 1 (2005): 75–91.

25. Rakesh Khurana, *From Higher Aims to Hired Hands: The Social Transformation of American Business Education and the Unfulfilled Promise of Management as a Profession* (Princeton, NJ: Princeton University Press, 2007).

26. Sheldon S. Wolin, *Democracy Incorporated* (Princeton, NJ: Princeton University Press, 2008).

# Five

# Board Governance Depends on Where You Sit

WILLIAM GEORGE

Board governance is a topic that is frequently discussed and often misunderstood. In this chapter, I offer an insiders' perspective on board governance. Over the years, I have had the privilege of serving on ten corporate boards, as well as being chairman and CEO of Medtronic, chairman only, and CEO only. I have also observed dozens of boards from outside the boardroom and have engaged in numerous confidential conversations with members of these boards about the challenges they faced and how they handled them.

What I have learned from these experiences is that one's perspective about the board's governance is strongly influenced by the seat one holds—whether one is an independent director, chair and CEO, CEO only, chair only, or someone who believes in governance but has never served on a major board. That's why it is essential to look at corporate governance through the eyes of each of these positions, as well as from the perspective of policy makers and the general public.

So-called governance experts, many of whom have never participated in an executive session of a major board, are exerting increasing power over boards through the combination of shareholder proposals, media articles, and legislative actions. Yet their proposals deal almost entirely with formal board processes and "check the box" criteria that generally have little to do with the substance of how boards operate.

In the past decade, there has been so much focus on failed boards that many people are surprised to learn that corporate boards have made great progress since the Enron scandals earlier in the decade. The power balance between CEOs and independent directors has been brought into alignment, enhanced by executive sessions of the board with and without the CEO present. The new generation of corporate CEOs is using its boards more effectively and sharing with them openly, while giving greater credence to their inputs. Yet the external efforts to limit the power of corporate boards continue unabated, with most external proposals only serving to weaken board performance with an excessive amount of ministerial details.

## The Independent Director's Perspective

Serving as an independent director is a much more difficult task— and even more important—than most observers realize. With new board governance regulations in place and rising expectations and criticism of corporate boards by outsiders, it is far more difficult to be an independent director now than it was in years past.

Many observers have worried that qualified people will not serve on boards. That has not been my experience. It's just that they won't serve on as many boards as in the past, which is appropriate given the time it takes to be an effective board member. There are valid reasons for directors not to spread themselves too thin.

The greatest challenge that independent directors face is to keep themselves fully informed about the company on whose board they serve. Independent directors typically engage with the company and its board six to eight times a year—more frequently if they serve on the audit committee or other special committees. Given strict enforcement of director independence, directors generally lack the wealth of knowledge about the industry or the nature of the business that senior executives of the firms have. Thus, they are faced with a significant problem of information asymmetry because management has far more information than independent directors can ever absorb.

The nine different boards on which I have served as an independent director include a wide range of industries, from financial services to oil and gas, pharmaceuticals, retail, outdoor lawn equipment, and large computers. In none of these instances did I have industry-specific knowledge, nor was it possible to learn the industry in great enough depth to contribute to the management discourse in a meaningful way.

Given these inherent limitations, what then should independent directors contribute? Beyond the legal requirements and fiduciary responsibilities that are inherent to board service, there are four principal areas where directors should provide leadership: (1) providing management with sound judgments about difficult issues, and asking probing questions that cause management and the CEO to look at their challenges from a different perspective, (2) being an advocate for sound board governance, (3) helping to ensure the effectiveness of the company's leadership team and its leadership succession plans, and (4) taking on leadership roles in crises.

### Offering Sound Judgment and Asking the Right Questions

Given the problem of information asymmetry, how can directors keep informed of the vital information they need to perform these roles? How can they provide management with sound judgments and ask probing questions? Here are a few fundamental ideas.

- Ensure that management provides a complete board book so directors can properly prepare in advance for the meeting.

This book should include copies of all presentations to be made at the upcoming board meeting, including confidential as well as nonconfidential material. However, directors should guard against management putting directors on "information overload" with more detailed information than they can reasonably be expected to absorb.

- The CEO should keep board members informed of important events between board meetings. This can be done with monthly progress reports, interim informational telephone meetings of the board, or individual telephone calls to all directors.

- Board meetings are most effective when they begin with an executive session with the CEO to update the board. In this session the CEO should review important events within the company and provide directors confidential opportunities to ask probing questions without having members of the management team present. The same objective can be accomplished by having a private dinner the night before the board meeting with the CEO, provided all directors are prepared to arrive early.

- Directors can also be kept informed between meetings by providing them with copies of relevant press articles and analysts' reports about the company.

Even in cases where all of these things are done well, as an independent director I often feel at a disadvantage in asking meaningful questions that will be helpful to the board and to management. In one instance I recall asking why the company wanted to implement an aggressive stock buyback program, when it might be better to preserve the cash to take advantage of opportunities or as a cushion if cash flow turned negative. My question was not well received by management. The CFO argued that the company had always been able to raise cash when it needed it and had never passed up an opportunity for lack of cash. A fellow director told me that I simply didn't understand the industry and that stock buybacks were routine. So I backed off.

However, a year later the company became so concerned about volatility in financial markets that it suspended all stock buybacks and began an aggressive program of increasing its liquidity. It was a good thing it had that wisdom, because the following year the markets completely shut down when the credit and liquidity crunch occurred. Had the firm not had a large cash reserve when that happened, it might have wound up insolvent like many of its competitors.

### Being an Advocate for Sound Board Governance

All independent directors need to be advocates of sound governance principles and ensure that the board follows its principles. This is especially important when things are not going well or the company is going through a crisis. Yet many directors tend to accept board governance as it is, without suggesting improvements in the process, and some even resist process improvements.

In the boardroom, process matters. It matters not just to abide by all governance rules. It matters because the process steps help ensure that all board members are engaged and fulfilling their responsibilities. More important, it ensures the proper balance of power between management and the board.

Perhaps the most useful aspect of the governance rules passed in 2003 is the executive session of the board *without* the CEO present. These sessions give directors the opportunity for sharing concerns about the company and asking for improved governance steps or additional reviews. They are also a time to discuss privately any concerns directors have about the management and whether they are being informed fully of the essential things they need to know to fulfill their obligations as directors. Finally, these sessions are useful in building chemistry among the independent directors.

One director of a major European company shared with me his frustration when he challenged the CEO and the direction in which he was moving the company and received no support—just silence—from his fellow directors. Later, when the board went into executive session without the CEO in the room, the directors went around the table and unanimously agreed with the first director, saying that the CEO was not providing the right leadership or taking the company on a sound course.

*Leadership Succession*

Nearly all independent directors say that their most important role is selecting the right leadership for the firm. Yet how much time do they actually devote to this vital task? In my experience, the time spent on leadership succession is far too limited and not nearly candid enough.

All too often board members settle for a contingency plan for replacing the leader—the "hit by a bus" scenario. Of course, when that happens, having a contingency plan for replacing the CEO is crucial, even if it is for an interim period. Not infrequently, the person identified will not be the best long-term successor, just the most obvious interim leader.

To prepare for succession, boards should have multiple discussions each year to identify long-term candidates to lead the firm in the next generation. They need to create ways to get to know these candidates personally and to observe how they react in crises and under pressure. This should include a series of assignments designed to prepare prospective candidates for the CEO role as well as other senior executive positions.

If the succession process is not taken seriously by both directors and the CEO, when the time comes to make the succession decision, directors may find that they do not have confidence in the internal candidates. Faced with this situation, directors may react— or overreact—by immediately initiating an external search, which bears substantial risks of its own. It is not uncommon to find that outside hires, although they look good on paper and have been successful elsewhere, do not understand the company's culture and values and do not take the time to find out who the people are that make the organization run successfully. Outsiders are prone to take aggressive actions in the short term that may be cheered by external observers but often have negative long-term consequences for the company's competitive posture.

Rather, the board should conduct detailed leadership succession planning sessions to review candidates and their progression within the management, ensuring that they have the necessary experiences to get them ready for the top jobs. In these reviews the age of the potential top leaders matters; they should not be so close in age to the CEO that they would be unable to have a sufficient tenure as CEO prior to reaching mandatory retirement. Nor can they be so young that there simply isn't time to have the experiences they need for such a major task. Thus, the process of identifying candidates for top roles must start early—typically, with leaders who are barely thirty years old.

On one board on which I served, the long-time CEO, who was doing an excellent job, steadfastly resisted the board's insistence that he develop potential successors. Frustrated by his inaction, the compensation committee (of which I was not a member) voted to provide him with a special bonus of several million dollars for grooming a prospective successor. He then reluctantly initiated an external search for a chief operating officer.

However, before any candidates were identified, he set up an off-site meeting with the independent directors to recommend that the external search be canceled because "it was causing too much disruption." Instead, he proposed to the board that he would develop some much younger candidates who were not only several years away but did not appear to have the long-term potential to become CEO.

That was enough for me. I decided to resign rather than being part of this charade. The CEO stayed for many more years, eventually stepping down after twenty-four years in the job. Even then, he continued to occupy his CEO office at company headquarters. His successor, who was quite junior to him, found that managers routinely took problems and opportunities to the old CEO, thereby undermining the new CEO's authority.

## Leading in Crisis

The real test of a board of directors occurs when the company is facing a crisis. Examples of crises that I have personally experienced include the termination or resignation of the CEO, an external financial crisis like the 2008 financial market meltdown, major governmental action against the firm, and an unexpected takeover attempt. In these situations board members need to understand and trust each other so that they can have candid conversations and ultimately reach consensus conclusions that have far-reaching implications for the company. Trust becomes even more important when the meeting is conducted by telephone, which is often the case in crises.

The time that independent directors are most counted upon to step up to their responsibilities is when an unexpected crisis hits the firm, as it inevitably will. Their accumulated wisdom and judgments are crucial to make sound decisions under the pressure of time and external media attention. It is often surprising to observe which directors take lead roles during a crisis. In crises, directors will find that the time requirements and personal inconvenience of board service escalate dramatically.

Such a crisis occurred on the Goldman Sachs board in 2006 when chair and CEO Henry Paulson was named Secretary of the Treasury by President Bush. Paulson called me and other directors on Memorial Day to inform us of his decision, which became public the next day. He also provided us with his succession recommendations. Given the public nature of this transition and the visibility of the firm, there were myriad media stories about what the board might do, most of them based on uninformed speculation. These circumstances greatly increased the pressure the board was under in making its decisions.

Fortunately, Paulson had laid the groundwork for this eventuality several years before by grooming multiple succession candidates and exposing them to the board through board presentations and informal meetings over lunch and dinner. In 2003 Lloyd Blankfein had been promoted to vice chairman; the following year he was named president and chief operating officer. Blankfein's promotion to chair and CEO was an obvious choice.

Goldman Sachs has always been a firm with shared power at the top of what used to be a partnership. After examining the many talented executives in the firm, the board elected Gary Cohn and Jon Winkelried as co-presidents and members of the board of directors. Had the board not been fully prepared for such a possibility and built such trust among the board members, it would not have been prepared to make such important decisions in such a limited period of time.

The bottom line for independent directors is that their responsibilities and obligations are so great these days that they cannot serve on a board and expect to preside while fulfilling the minimum requirements. Rather, they need to be fully engaged, learn the business, and stay connected between meetings. Otherwise, they won't be prepared to lead when a crisis hits.

## The Perspective of a CEO with a Nonexecutive Chair

In 1991 I became CEO of Medtronic, two years after joining the company as president and chief operating officer. My predecessor, who had just turned sixty-five, continued as chair of the board. I was quite satisfied to have him in this role. He had a wealth of experience and wisdom that were very valuable to me as CEO, and he had the full confidence of the board. He was also more than willing to take on difficult assignments at my request regarding delicate government and legal issues.

This structure, with two different people as CEO and nonexecutive chair, is preferred by most governance experts and some regulators and is the standard European model. The split responsibilities clearly separate the role of management (to lead the company) from that of the board chair (to take responsibility for the board and governance).

As obvious as this dual structure seems, the benefits of separating the board chair position from that of the CEO is not supported by research demonstrating that split roles create superior performance. To date, there is no evidence that this structure does so, or even that it provides greater stability at the top. Anecdotally, the opposite is often the case.

In reality, the effectiveness of the dual structure depends on the relationship between the two individuals in these roles. If they are not squarely in agreement about the direction of the company, its leadership, and its strategy, an unhealthy separation may emerge, both within the board and between management and the board. This can result in a lack of clear direction for the company. As a result, malaise or confusion may develop within the employee ranks that can easily spread to customers, shareholders, and other interested parties.

In the worst case, the two leaders engage in a power struggle that winds up paralyzing the company and both its management and the board. This struggle can prevent the company from making important decisions and render it incapable of responding to market and strategic changes in a timely manner. Several years ago just such a split occurred on the British Petroleum board that led to years of conflict until the CEO ultimately resigned and a new, independent board chair was appointed a year later.

As much as I supported the separate roles in my initial phase as CEO, I found that over time this arrangement became more difficult. For example, some board members seemed confused about who they should look to for strategic direction, especially in the case of acquisitions. In addition, the chair felt he should be "the eyes and ears of the board" within the company. Over time this led to some confusion within management about his role. The board was also somewhat confused about whether I reported to him or to the board as a whole, an issue that was never fully clarified. Quite naturally, I felt that I reported to the board as a whole, and that my responsibility and authority to lead the company depended on those relationships.

Although it would seem that having the two positions held by different people would ease the time burdens of the CEO's job, I learned that in reality the opposite was the case. I had to spend a great deal of time involved in board governance and in responding to issues raised by the board.

There was also a tension that developed because board members seemed hesitant to give me direct feedback or to talk openly about concerns that they and other board members had. When I also became board chair, this tension evaporated quickly, and I found myself spending far less time on board governance. In part, this was because communication lines opened up and were more direct.

In recent years it has become much more common among U.S. corporations for a new CEO *not* to be named board chair initially. Instead, either the former CEO continues as board chair, as was the case at Medtronic, or one of the current board members takes on the added role of nonexecutive chair. This transition period can work well to provide seamless transitions at the top and to let new CEOs get their bearings before taking on the challenges of board governance.

## The Perspective of the Chair and CEO

American CEOs strongly prefer the dual mandate of being board chair as well as CEO. They believe it puts them squarely in charge of both management and the board and avoids the likelihood of conflicts or power struggles within the boardroom. In the past, however, this has often led to complacency on the part of the board and a tendency not to get deeply involved until it is too late to avoid difficult situations. This possibility is increased by the information asymmetry problem.

These days these relationships are rapidly changing. The new NYSE governance rules, enacted at the time of Sarbanes-Oxley, have done a great deal to rebalance the power between the CEO and the board. As a result, independent directors are taking their responsibilities very seriously. With the rising use of lead directors representing the independent directors, the differences between a nonexecutive board chair and lead director have been greatly narrowed. If lead directors take their responsibilities seriously, the differences may be more a matter of external appearance and form than substance.

Effective leaders with the dual mandate keep their independent directors well informed through a combination of telephone updates, monthly progress reports, and candid comments in executive sessions with the independent directors about the real-time issues the company is facing. They are responsive to the concerns raised by independent directors and either take action on them or put them on the board agenda for discussion by the full board.

They are also respectful of the directors' need for independence and for having open discussions without the CEO present to ensure that important issues are talked through privately. That is why many experienced board members believe that the most important process improvement in the past decade has been the requirement for independent directors to meet regularly in executive session without the CEO or other nonindependent directors present. These confidential discussions have led to a more open and unified process than existed previously.

The rise of the role of lead director, elected by the independent directors only, is also contributing to a better separation of governance from management. To make the position of lead director work effectively, it is essential that there be a separate job description for this role, one that is publicly available and respected by the chair and CEO. The most effective lead directors see this role as someone who is "first among equals" and can coordinate the opinions of all directors and facilitate open discussion among them.

In my case I became chair and CEO of Medtronic after serving for five years as CEO when my predecessor retired from the board at age seventy. I found that having the dual positions clarified a great deal for the board about who they should look to for leadership and strategic direction, and in the midst of difficult issues. When the opportunity to do a series of acquisitions in 1998 that ultimately transformed the company became apparent, the board was unified in proceeding.

Nevertheless, lodging both roles in a single person is filled with challenges. Having served on several boards with a single leader in the combined roles of chair and CEO, I have learned that the board is most effective when the leader clearly understands the difference between these two roles and leans over backward to respect the independence of the board.

An individual serving as combined chair and CEO needs to develop consciously the skills to handle both roles simultaneously. He or she has to facilitate open discussions on the board while at the same time representing management's position to the board. If the individual argues his or her case too strenuously, he or she may shut down thoughtful comments from the independent directors. On the other hand, if the individual acts solely as a facilitator of these discussions, he or she will not be giving directors the full benefit of management's thinking and rationale.

When I had this dual role, I did whatever I could to open up meaningful discussions within the board, especially by drawing out the opinions of quieter members of the board. This was especially challenging when the board was discussing important strategic issues or acquisitions and needed the benefit of my judgments and insights. My tendency had been to be quite forceful in offering opinions. I had to learn to withhold them until others had the opportunity to offer theirs and then work them into the context of my conclusions. Not infrequently, this meant holding off on making decisions until the board had some time to digest the ideas or management could undertake additional analyses.

One of the benefits the board and I had was an active, capable lead director with whom I could work closely. He did a superb job in guiding the issues of the independent directors and in keeping me fully informed of any concerns and issues the board might have. When it came time to select my successor, he was especially effective in developing a sound process that we agreed upon, and then leading the board through it. He gets a great deal of credit for the seamless transition that occurred when I concluded my ten-year term and my successor took over.

At Target, the differences between the roles were emphasized by splitting the chair and CEO's bonus into two parts, each with a separate board evaluation. Seventy percent of the weight was given to performance as CEO and 30 percent to performance as board chair. It was not uncommon for these evaluations to differ significantly within a given year. This process provided board members the opportunity to provide differential feedback; for example, your feedback could be positive about an individual's performance as CEO, while raising concerns about board governance and important issues not being addressed at the board level.

## The Perspective of a Board Chair Who Is Not a CEO

The role of board chairs may depend heavily on the experience they bring to this position. Are they former CEOs of the company or of another company? Were they members of the board before becoming chair? Is their background in leadership or has their experience been primarily as a sophisticated adviser, such as a lawyer or financial expert? Is this an ongoing role, or are they there just for an interim period?

If they were the prior CEO—a not uncommon situation—board chairs will bring a wealth of experience to their role, a keen knowledge of the other directors, some strong opinions about what the company needs, and oftentimes a legacy to nourish or at least maintain. Therein lies the difficulty: no matter how hard they try to constrain themselves, they may have a tendency to overshadow or, even worse, override the new CEO.

This problem may be accentuated by independent directors who still rely heavily on their opinions and may trust them more than they do the new CEO's recommendations. Still, if the former CEOs can restrain themselves and also recognize that it is time to let go and do everything they can to support their successors, they can be very effective in this role. Often, it helps if they devote themselves to other activities in which they can continue to use their leadership abilities.

In my case at Medtronic, I was committed to a seamless transition with my successor and to ensuring his success and the company's. Also, the board and I had agreed upon a timetable of just one year for me to serve as chair, so I was clearly in a transitional mode. I was still in my fifties and looking forward to turning my attention to other interests. I had already accepted a dual appointment (that would begin shortly before the end of my tenure as board chair) as professor of leadership and governance at two Swiss academic centers, one the top Swiss technological institution and the other one of Europe's leading private business schools.

Nevertheless, it didn't take long before the new CEO and I faced a board challenge in this regard. It came at an off-site board meeting in Switzerland just a month after the transition of the CEO role. For fifteen years, dating back to my predecessor's tenure, Medtronic had pursued externally announced goals of 15 percent per annum growth in both revenues and profits, compounded over any five-year period. These aggressive goals provided great discipline within the company and a consistent benchmark for shareholders. We had been quite successful in exceeding these goals, but not without a lot of risks and challenges.

One of the independent directors argued forcefully that given the company's larger size, it would be impossible to continue to achieve such high rates of growth. I was tempted to jump into the discussion and defend the importance of these goals, but somehow held my fire. Fortunately, my successor held firm in spite of the temptation to accept lower goals of 10 to 12 percent growth. He also turned to the CFO to provide an oral analysis of the impact on the stock price of lower goals, which he estimated to be a decline of 50 percent or more. As a result, the company stayed on the same aggressive course, and its growth exceeded 15 percent growth in both revenues and earnings for the next six years as well.

Many people argue with sound logic that the former CEO is not the right person to serve as board chair and that he should leave the board immediately. An alternate choice could be one of the existing directors, provided there is a well-qualified candidate on the board with the time available to serve in this role. This choice can work, provided the board member is primarily interested in ensuring the continuity of the firm and doesn't get into competition with the CEO. An equally good choice is to appoint someone who has served as chair or CEO or both of another company and has the time and inclination to take on such a role.

In certain countries such as Switzerland, the board chair may be an independent attorney or financial expert. Although this solution looks good on paper because of the absence of conflicts, in practice it may not work that well because someone who has never run a company may not have sufficient knowledge of the company, its business, and what it takes to lead the company.

To ensure that the role of nonexecutive board chair is an accountable position, it must have a well-defined job description. The nonexecutive chair should be formally evaluated at least annually by fellow board members. Finally, the position should have a defined time period, after which a new nonexecutive chair is elected or this person is formally reelected.

# Reflections on the Importance of Role Perspective

There is merit in the diversity of perspectives that board members have, based on their role on the board. Given the importance of these multiple perspectives, how should boards ensure that the differences are understood and taken into account in board decisions? Here are some suggestions:

- The board should acknowledge that there is no single structure that works in all cases. In this regard it should be pragmatic enough to adapt to the individuals involved rather than fixing in place a rigid structure.

- It is important that all parties, especially the CEO, acknowledge these different points of view and work to minimize inherent conflicts that emanate from the perspective that comes from one's position. This requires high-level listening skills, the ability to see situations from the other person's perspective, and the wisdom to understand the basis for their different points of view.

- All directors, especially the CEO, can benefit from holding these different positions, either within the company or on other boards of directors. In this regard the nominating committee of the board should seek out prospective board members who have served as CEO or board chair or both in other companies. The board should also encourage its CEOs to serve on at least one outside board to enable them to have the experience of being an independent director and to understand the challenges that independent directors face.

If these basic guidelines are followed, I believe that board governance will improve markedly. As a result, companies will have the steady hand in the boardroom that will enable them to sustain their success through successive generations of leadership and board membership.

# Six

# Recognizing Negative Boardroom Group Dynamics

KATHARINA PICK
AND KENNETH MERCHANT

Group dynamics—the interactions, interpersonal relationships, and patterns of behavior that occur in a group—shape the ways in which groups perform in any setting. Group dynamics certainly affect boards of directors, the group situated at the head of every organization. Some group dynamics are positive, such that board members can inform, challenge, and stimulate each other. But other dynamics are negative. Even when boards are composed of highly accomplished, experienced, and mostly well-meaning individuals, as they commonly are, boards are just as likely to succumb to the potentially negative sides of group behavior as any other group.

This chapter discusses what we believe to be the most relevant, most important types of negative group dynamics—or pathologies—that can undermine a board's ability to provide effective oversight. The pathologies we discuss can overlap, but they are distinct phenomena and are individually observable and identifiable. Our primary focus, however, is on remedies for these pathologies. We discuss how board leaders and individual board members can and should act to minimize the effects of these pathologies. The challenges are considerable, because ameliorating one group pathology often triggers or exacerbates another.

Perhaps because so many recent governance failures occurred in boards that *seemed,* from the outside, to be well positioned for success, researchers have focused more attention on understanding what happens *inside* boardrooms in the last ten years than in prior decades.[1] Enron's board, for example, boasted a stellar group of experts in diverse areas. Its directors were highly qualified; they had significant ownership stakes; the board and its committees met regularly and appeared to be well structured; and directors were satisfied with their meetings, materials, and the internal board relations.[2] But something went seriously wrong. No doubt there were some failures of individual Enron board members, and maybe even misconduct. But it is equally likely that the Enron failure, and others like it, can be traced to some destructive board dynamics that undermined the abilities of well-intentioned board members to provide good corporate oversight.

Can effective board leadership and processes minimize the effects of the pathologies enough that boards can be said to be providing effective oversight? Probably. However, not all corporate governance experts and critics are convinced. The severity of the challenges has caused some to question whether the unitary board structure that predominates in the United States can be relied upon to provide effective corporate oversight. We offer some reflections on this at the end of the chapter.

# Universal Board Process Best Practices

Decades of governance research—as well as legal reforms and activism by shareholder groups—have led to important reforms in how boards function. Today, there are accepted best practices on a variety of dimensions. To some extent, good board practices can avoid or at least minimize these pathologies. We assume that these best practices are a foundation upon which other aspects of board process are built. A partial list of generally agreed upon best practices includes the following:

- *Board Composition and Size.* Boards of directors should be composed of members with a good mix of specialized expertise, including knowledge of the industry, customers, and important management functions. The board members should have diverse perspectives and opinions. The board should not be too large or too small. If the board is too large, it is more difficult for individual directors to become actively involved in the discussions. If the board is too small, it is difficult to have all the requisite knowledge and abilities at hand, and the workload might be too great for directors to perform effectively. In the United States, the most common board size is ten directors. Most board members should be independent of management, as regulations now require.

- *Board Member Behavior.* Boards should be composed solely of members who are energetic, inquisitive, and attentive—with time to perform their duties. They should stay well informed about the developments in their company's industry. They should be willing to express their opinions in meetings in constructive ways.

- *Board Leadership.* The independent board must control the agenda and conduct of the board meetings, not management. Depending on the situation, this can be done effectively either by an independent board chair or a lead independent director (see chapters 7 and 8). The leader should establish orderly processes and encourage all the individual directors to stay properly engaged, to contribute their knowledge and opinions freely, and to work toward a consensus.

- *Board Committees.* The board should delegate some discussions to committees. The committee structure allows for discussion of certain issues in more detail by board members with specialized expertise. Care must be taken to ensure that communications between committees and the full board are effective.

- *Role Clarity.* Directors must understand and agree on their board's role, both legal and practical, particularly on issues involving relationships and separations of duties with management. The board members must also understand their individual responsibilities. They need to understand the unique areas of expertise that they bring to the board and the areas of expertise of the other board members. They also need to understand when they should forcefully argue their positions rather than accede to others' judgments.

- *Board Evaluations.* The board should evaluate itself and its individual members regularly. Feedback from the evaluations should be used to improve the board composition, structures, and processes as necessary.

## Board Tensions and Trade-offs

As boards enact these various best practices and try to achieve an effective group process, they face a set of unavoidable tensions or trade-offs. Leaders of all groups must contend with these tensions. Not managing them appropriately can lead to pathologies, or problematic group functioning, in even the most perfectly designed boards. As will become clear, managing the tensions can be a fluid process and often more of an art than a clearly delineated set of tasks. Simply recognizing the tensions is an important first step for any board leader. Six tensions inherent in the functioning of every group that are particularly challenging and relevant for boards of directors are discussed in this section.

## The Social-Cohesion Tension

One tension that boards face is between creating social cohesion and avoiding it. *Social cohesion* refers to the total field of forces that bind a group of individuals together and keep members wanting to be part of the group. Factors may include attraction, common interests, cultural similarity, and social ties, among many others.[3] Strong social cohesion in the board allows it to function smoothly, keeps directors motivated, and helps the group cope with internal conflict and politicking.

However, social cohesion can also heighten pressures of conformity in the group. Groups are notoriously powerful in creating social pressures to conform even when group members are performing an easy task, but this is especially true when the task is difficult and ambiguous, as the most important work of the board is. The more socially cohesive the group, the greater the pressure for any member to conform to the majority's point of view. Conformity can prevent useful bits of information and opinions from surfacing and, at the extreme, can lead to the very dangerous group dynamic called groupthink.

To avoid destructive conflict while simultaneously guarding against conformity and groupthink, a board must develop a degree of social cohesion, but not too much. The choice is not between cohesion and no cohesion. Rather, the questions are *how much* cohesion and *of what types?*

## The Dissension Tension

A second tension is the degree to which dissent should be allowed to exist or even be encouraged in board discussions. On the one hand, dissent or simply expressing an alternative viewpoint is critical to avoiding conformity. Research shows that merely having considered a minority viewpoint allows a group to think more creatively and make better decisions.[4] Dissent can also prevent groups from falling into stultifying habitual routines that can both obscure problems and prevent effective responses. Rather than applying past behaviors to a current situation, dissent can help the group reevaluate its course of action. Finally, disciplined or forced dissent can force new information onto the table that otherwise might not become available to the group.

However, too much dissent can create conflict, undermine the aforementioned social cohesion of the group, and simply stall meetings. Trying to find the appropriate balance and the right manner in which to encourage dissent are two of the most important tasks for anyone leading a board discussion. Some tension in the boardroom is good; too much can lead to infighting and chaos. The goal should be to create friendly, constructive dissension.

### The Psychological-Safety Tension

Group psychological safety is the shared belief that the group is a safe place for risk taking, sharing unpopular ideas, and admitting errors.[5] Some degree of psychological safety is essential. When a group provides psychological safety, members are more likely to speak up, to ask questions, and to admit mistakes, all of which are important to other group outcomes, such as decision making and learning. Having psychological safety counteracts conformity pressures and groupthink, and can keep a group from following an unexamined habitual routine.

However, too much safety creates a tendency toward social loafing. Social loafing occurs when individuals engaged in a collective task exert less effort than they would if they were performing this task alone.[6] It is a well-documented phenomenon that occurs in both trivial and serious situations, with many different kinds of tasks. The causes of social loafing have to do with identifiability. When an individual believes that his or her effort will not be noticed or rewarded, he or she is inclined to loaf. A corollary is that when an individual believes his or her reduced effort will not be noticed, he or she will loaf. This is particularly true for less skilled, or less confident, group members and for people who do not find the task intrinsically rewarding. Although we would hope that directors are intrinsically motivated to fulfill their board duties, it is unlikely that every aspect of board work is experienced this way and by all directors. Accountability and visibility become important issues. Very importantly, directors need to believe that their input is valued, identifiable, and evaluated. In other words, board members must feel both psychological safety and accountability. How this can be achieved is discussed in the pages ahead.

## The Collectivist-Feelings Tension

To avoid destructive conflict, politicking, and dysfunctional coalition formation, the board needs to have a sense of being a group—a collective engaged in a joint task. Board members must have a level of agreement about the group's role in governance, and they must cooperate to gain the advantages of being a group. But if the board allows this collectivist feeling to override the uniqueness and visibility of individual directors, social loafing can become a problem. Moreover, if the collectivist feeling begins to override the need for dissent, the conformity issues discussed earlier also come into play. It is critical, therefore, to create a balance between operating and feeling like a collective and still valuing and measuring individual contributions.

## The Diversity-of-Thought Tension

Related to the previous tension is the proper extent of diversity in board composition. The more diverse a board is, the less likely it is to be highly socially cohesive, which leads to the benefits and drawbacks discussed previously (e.g., less conformity and groupthink, more dissent). Greater diversity can help to improve board decision making by providing the board with more varied knowledge and information. In particular, this can help a board avoid the phenomenon of group polarization. Group polarization happens when a group collectively makes a more extreme decision than the individual directors would have chosen to make individually. In other words, the collective decision does not accurately reflect the average of the individual decisions. When more varied, concrete, and relevant information is available for discussion a group is less likely to suffer from this problem.

On the flip side, diversity can be a detriment because there is likely to be less *shared* information among group members. Groups typically spend most of their time considering information that is shared rather than held by only one or two members of the group. Because of this tendency, great diversity can also be a detriment to board decision making. Again, the trick is to find the balance and to manage these tendencies that are related to different degrees of diversity.

### The Strong-Leader Tension

Finally, there is the matter of board leadership. Board leaders, either chairs or lead independent directors, have important roles to fill. They must lead the board's activities. They must shape the board meeting norms and culture, set the agendas, and frame the issues appropriately. At times they must be firm and not allow, for example, time to be wasted or dissension to get out of control. At times, they might have to help the board confront the CEO and other members of top management on important issues.

But board leaders must also not be too firm. They must be careful not to alienate directors or to upset the balance of power in a "group of equals." They must encourage each individual board member to contribute his or her knowledge and perspectives. When the issues are important, they must allow adequate time for those contributions to emerge, even if, at times, they consume significant portions of the available meeting time. And, of course, the board leaders must be careful not to exploit their power in an effort to have their opinions prevail. Although convictions can be strong, the board must govern as a collective. So again, there is an inherent tension: boards need strong leadership, but not too strong.

# The Pathologies

When the tensions just discussed are either unacknowledged or are balanced inappropriately, a number of problematic dynamics—or pathologies—may occur. In this section we define each of the nine pathologies and describe how each relates to the five tensions.[7]

## Excessive Conformity

Excessive conformity occurs particularly in groups that are dealing with ambiguous information, as boards often do. A tendency toward conformity is an aspect of life in all groups, because group members often feel pressure to go along with the majority viewpoint in the group. The conformity becomes excessive when it leads to poor decision making. The desire to conform can prevent individuals from bringing relevant expertise and information to the group work.

Groupthink is a form of excessive conformity with some unique features. Groups that fall into it develop a sense of invulnerability—sometimes based on their own past success—that drives group members to make the survival of the group the number one priority. The group may question or shield itself from disconfirming information. Members become loyal to the group and create and feel tremendous pressure to conform to the majority viewpoint. The risk that such conformity will affect board process is increased when there is high social cohesion, when there are norms that prevent dissension, when psychological safety and collectivist feelings are high, and when there is little diversity on the board.

## Negative Group Conflict

Moderate amounts of task conflict, or conflict that stems from resources, judgments, or procedures related to a particular task, is actually beneficial for groups. However, relational conflict, which is based on differences in values or interpersonal styles, almost always harms the functioning of the group.[8] Any group that experiences too much of either type of conflict will likely suffer some disabling effects. Negative conflict is most likely to occur when social cohesion is low, dissension is frequent, psychological safety and collectivist feelings are low, and the board is very diverse. Although a strong board leader may not ensure that negative conflict will not happen, a weak board leader almost certainly guarantees that it will.

## Politicking and Dysfunctional Coalition Formation

This is how we refer to the negative side of power tactics. It is impossible to imagine a board operating without the use of power by those in the group who have it in any given situation. However, manipulative uses of power, which can involve complex maneuverings and blindsiding, destroy group trust and undermine effective group processes going forward. Keeping power from taking on these destructive forms is difficult but important, particularly for boards, which are usually populated with people accustomed to having and exercising power.

Use of negative power tactics is most likely to occur when social cohesion is low, when dissension is suppressed, and when psychological safety and collectivist feelings are weak. It is perhaps too simple to say that diversity increases the use of negative power tactics, but, depending on how the diversity is distributed and handled, there may be greater opportunity or impulse for coalition forming in more diverse groups. In regard to the board leadership, having a weak board leader, or a void of leadership, almost surely will contribute to the use of more subversive power tactics as directors try to get things done.

## Habitual Routines

Habitual routines are the aspects of the group process that have become excessively routinized over time. Instead of reassessing the appropriateness of a routine, groups proceed mindlessly and effortlessly through a particular routine. Although routines can create efficiencies, they can become problematic when the group does not accurately assess whether the routine is appropriate for the specific situations it is facing. Boards that are most likely to fall into habitual routines that do not suit the situation are those on which dissension and psychological safety are low. Social cohesion, collectivist feelings, diversity, and board leadership may play out either way, depending on how they interact with the other tensions. For example, if high social cohesion helps to create psychological safety, then its effect on habitual routines could be favorable.

## Shared Information Bias

Shared information bias is the tendency for groups to spend the most time and consideration on information that is shared by most of the group members, rather than on information that may be more important or valuable but is held by only one or two members in the group. This bias can create some harmful misconceptions and blind spots.

## Pluralistic Ignorance

Another form of cognitive bias, pluralistic ignorance occurs when individual members of a group do not voice an opinion because they assume it to be very different from the majority of other group members. In keeping quiet, they never realize that many or even all of the other group members actually share their opinion. Pluralistic ignorance can lead to outcomes that none, or very few, of the individual members actually wanted. Shared information bias and pluralistic ignorance are most likely to occur when dissension is low, psychological safety is low, and when board leadership is weak. Social cohesion, collectivist feeling, and diversity may again play out in either direction depending on the other features of the board.

## Social Loafing

Social loafing is the phenomenon by which individuals exert less effort on a task while they are working as part of a team than they would if they were working alone. It is a variation of the "free rider" problem often discussed in group incentive settings and has been shown to occur in many kinds of measurable group tasks. Social loafing is most likely to occur when psychological safety and collectivist feelings are high, when diversity is low, and when there is no strong board leadership. Social cohesion and dissension may move loafing in either direction depending on the other factors.

### Group Polarization

Group polarization occurs when a group makes a decision collectively that is more extreme than the members would have made had their individual votes simply been tallied. It often happens naturally in a group setting. When the group votes after discussion, the mean of opinions tends to shift in the direction the group initially leaned, but in an extreme fashion. Group polarization is most likely to occur when dissension is low, when psychological safety is low, when the board is not diverse, and when board leadership is weak or nonexistent. Social cohesion and collectivist feelings may affect this pathology in either direction.

## Managing the Inherent Trade-offs and Tensions

The best way to minimize the incidence of these pathologies and their effects is to manage the five tensions we discussed earlier. Several steps are important here.

First, it must be determined who should assume responsibility for management of the board. Boards are mostly a group of equals, with minimum hierarchy and fewer differentiated roles than we see in top-management teams. Each individual board member has a fiduciary responsibility to the firm and its shareholders. Because of this equality, board group process may wander far afield without any single board member charged with the responsibility to manage it.

Where there is an independent chair of the board, it is clear that that person must assume responsibility for overseeing the board's processes. Equally clear is that when the board has someone serving in a combined chairman/CEO role, given the potential for conflicts of interest, responsibility for the board processes must be assumed by the lead outside director. This latter situation can be challenging if the CEO/chair, not the lead director, is running the meetings. In such cases, it is even more imperative for individual board members to realize whether and when their boards are in a pathological group situation and to exercise their legal authority and responsibility to intervene.

Second, the board leaders and members must apply the generic knowledge of the tensions and pathologies that we have discussed earlier to their specific board and company situation. What are the most likely and potentially most destructive negative board dynamics threats? Is the board a prime example of a social club, with strong social cohesion, many long-term friendships, and strong mutual affection among the board members? This might call for awareness or rebalancing efforts to avoid the potential for groupthink. Or is the board a group of individuals assembled by an executive search firm, with no overlapping career paths or prior acquaintances? Is the potential for destructive conflict high, and might the board benefit from a shift toward more social cohesion? Has the board operated in a period of calm and relative success with very little turnover in board membership? Has the board developed some habitual routines that could hinder its ability to assess and respond to changing competitive conditions? Any of these situations might call for a rebalancing in some of the areas of tension. The board leader might encourage more dissension as a regular course of board discussion, or the board could, over the longer term, attempt to increase diversity.

Related questions that boards should be asking themselves are as follows: What are the consequences for the company of each of the pathologies that are possible? Which end of the spectrum of any of the tensions just discussed would be more detrimental to the board and company? What would happen if the situation were left unchanged? Would the board tend to move to one of the extremes?

The right balance in each area of tension will be different for each board, depending on the nature of the personalities in the room, the style of the board leader, the condition of the enterprise, and the competitive environment. The balance may also change—or have to change—when institutional expectations of boards change. For example, in recent years there has been an unrelenting emphasis on director independence and all of the definitions of independence one can imagine. It is more difficult for a board, in these times, to assemble a group of directors who are linked by other directorships, by prior work experience, or socially. How does this factor into social cohesion? Are there things boards need to incorporate into their process today that were not necessary twenty years ago?

Third, decisions must be made as to how to manage each of the tensions. Is it best to walk a center line in any specific tension area, forgoing some benefits but also avoiding some potential pitfalls, or is it best to move toward one end of a tension spectrum because it is more important given the board's current circumstance or makeup? If choices have to be made between one of two evils, which should be chosen? Should any structural changes be made? Should the board composition, meeting calendar, and/or meeting formats and styles be changed?

Managing board social dynamics is an important part of being both an effective board leader and an effective board member. It is an important and never-ending task.

## The Individual Board Member's Role in Group Process

The majority of this chapter has focused on how we might avoid certain group pathologies on boards, with the assumption that we actually have control over them. A number of directors will likely think our suggestions are unrealistic given the politics inside their own boardrooms. You may wonder how you, as one individual director, can influence board process when others are not tuned in or do not think it is particularly important. Even more complicated is the situation in which you are the lone director on a board dominated by a very powerful chairman/CEO (or other dominant directors) who is not eager to discuss such matters as board process. If your board is venturing into groupthink, for example, how can you as an individual with no formal power intervene in the downward spiral in a way that does not make you an outcast or cost you your board seat?

We have some advice for individual directors. The best time to evaluate how effectively a board is paying attention to process is when you are joining. Speaking with the chairman can be particularly informative. How does he or she run board meetings? How does he or she judge whether a meeting has been effective? How does he or she define the chair role? It is also useful to consider the board evaluation process. On what measures does the board as a whole give and receive feedback? Are there any process components to the evaluation? Are directors evaluated individually? Are the suggestions acted upon?

If you are already on the board, it may be more difficult to shape your board's fate. But there are still things you can do. One of the most important is to help create an environment for positive dissent. Voicing minority opinions is perhaps the single most effective safeguard against conformity and poor decision making. Introducing comments with the phrase "Let me play the devil's advocate role here for a minute" takes the edge off dissenting comments. Some boards have actually benefited from appointing certain board members as temporary devil's advocates or bringing outsiders in to play that role in certain critical situations.

Another approach that is often nonthreatening to the chairman is to frame questions as "naïve" and to preface comments as reflecting a "desire to learn." One might say, "Help me to understand this scenario/client/acquisition detail." Alternatively, claiming some part of the question can make it more palatable. For example, "Help me understand why we believe company X is the best target." Being willing to ask a question, even for lack of understanding, may be important to getting the board clued in on its process.

The responses to this type of questioning can be quite informative. Is the question ignored? Who responds? At the very least, other directors will have been party to an interaction that can cause reflection. Even better is that simply having someone walk through the rationale of a particular decision or discussion point may reveal flaws or open the door for others to raise concerns they may have. If the culture in the boardroom is so deeply entrenched against this kind of discussion, perhaps it would be more appropriate to ask the questions outside the boardroom. In this case, it still benefits the chairman or CEO or both to explain the thinking and the assumptions behind the issue.

Asking open-ended questions of other board members is another tactic that could create a safe climate for possible dissent. "Has anyone around this table worked with a client like this before?" Simply getting a discussion flowing can allow ideas to surface in a way that does not necessarily feel like dissent but does get alternative viewpoints to come forward. We have already mentioned that once a minority viewpoint is considered the ultimate outcome for the group discussion is more creative and more carefully reasoned.[9] Helping to make this kind of discussion available through "safe" forms of dissent is a critical tool for any individual board member. An additional benefit of asking other board members about their experiences is that it opens the door for directors to learn how their experiences are relevant to the board and test in a safe way how they might bring unique contributions that other directors cannot.

Another difficult challenge faced by individual board members is contending with a coalition of directors that has formed over the life of the board, through prior social and professional ties, or through some shared functional background. Time constraints often make it challenging for directors to spend much meaningful time with one another. But it is important that directors get a clear sense of who each person is, what he or she brings to the board in terms of professional expertise, and how he or she thinks about board work. Some of this can be gleaned from board discussions, but individual directors should make a point to connect and find areas of overlap with other board members. Nothing is more disempowering than being in a group where a limited set of individuals seem to congregate and dominate the course of discussion or group agenda. Directors must resist the urge to sit "solo" on their boards. Everyone must recognize their governance role as a "collective" activity. Despite being new, or different in some way, they must not become marginalized by informal social norms that emerge, whether they be fixed seating or speaking patterns or any other aspect of board processes. Creating and nurturing overlap with each board member is a way both of *creating* necessary social cohesion and *fighting* too much inappropriate social cohesion.

Finally, although this is covered earlier, when possible an individual director should encourage fellow board members to reflect on the process of the board. Perhaps this is best done in executive sessions or on board evaluations. A good board evaluation should have some space for directors to consider the *process* of how the group is working together. It may be easy to argue against taking precious board time to talk about such matters. However, the potential payoffs of doing so—or dangers of not doing so—are great.

## Conclusion

To be able to manage board processes effectively, board leaders and members must first understand the pathologies, their symptoms, and their causes. This chapter has provided only a brief introduction to this subject.

The pathologies of board social dynamics discussed in this chapter are real. They might be a primary cause of nearly every corporate governance failure, of which many have been in evidence in the last decade. What makes dealing with these pathologies so problematic is that the full set of them cannot be extinguished. Eliminating one pathology often makes another one more prominent. The reality is that managing the dynamics of the board is a constant balancing act to keep things in alignment so that the board is effective in meeting the most important requirements of its current circumstance.

Given that these negative social dynamics are a threat in every boardroom, should society trust groups of individuals (i.e., boards) to perform the critical corporate governance roles they have been given? There are not many options. Certainly no single individual could fulfill the entire role. No individual has the needed breadth of expertise or the time to perform all the needed oversight tasks effectively. Plus, absolute power is easily corrupted.

Some critics have suggested that a single unitary board, which is what is relied upon in the United States, cannot fulfill the role effectively either. They have called instead for a more complex model of corporate governance that is generally referred to by the rubric "network governance." Network governance uses two, or maybe more, boards with overlapping responsibilities to introduce a separation of powers between boards, and resulting checks and balances to provide protection against many of the pathologies discussed here. Multiple boards have more time and information processing capability than does a single board. Multiple boards can use competing communication channels and introduce broader sources of information, including, probably, more from parties that oppose the views of management. Boards with overlapping responsibilities would facilitate the cross checking of all information they receive, both from management and from other sources. Network governance can institutionalize into the governance system individuals who would otherwise be described as dissidents or whistle blowers. It makes it more likely both that decisions will be considered from all angles and that potential failures and excessive risks will be anticipated and discussed.

Working examples of network governance can be found. Before it went public, Visa International, which represented 22,000 member institutions, used multiple boards of directors within its single legal entity. These boards had irrevocable authority over specific geographic or functional areas.[10] Among other things, they hired, reviewed, and fired executives and approved projects and pricing. Some companies, such as public utilities, use various forms of stakeholder (e.g., customer, employee, community) councils for board advisory purposes. The German labor codetermination system and some aspects of Japanese keiretsu provide some network governance functions.

Of course, network governance is not a panacea either. The needed coordination mechanisms make the governance processes more costly, and network governance increases the potential for conflicts that would need to be resolved. Discussing all the various network governance alternatives and their advantages and disadvantages is beyond the scope of this chapter. It should be noted, however, that if unitary corporate boards cannot effectively address the social dynamics pathologies that were discussed in this chapter, legislatures and regulators might take away much of their power to provide oversight.

# Notes

1. R. Leblanc and J. Gillies, *Inside the Boardroom: How Boards Really Work and the Coming Revolution in Corporate Governance* (Mississauga, Ontario: John Wiley & Sons Canada, 2005); K. A. Merchant and K. Pick, *Blind Spots, Biases and Other Pathologies in the Boardroom* (New York: Business Expert Press, 2010).

2. L. J. Brooks and P. Dunn, *Business and Professional Ethics for Directors, Executives and Accountants,* 5th ed. (Mason, OH: South Western Cengage Learning, 2009), 72.

3. L. Festinger, S. Schachter, and K. W. Back, *Social Pressures in Informal Groups: A Study of Human Factors in Housing* (New York: Harper, 1950), 164.

4. C. Nemeth, "Differential Contributions of Majority vs. Minority Influence," *Psychological Review* 93, no. 1 (1986): 23–32.

5. A. Edmondson, "Psychological Safety and Learning in Work Teams," *Administrative Science Quarterly* 44 (1999): 350–383.

6. S. J. Karau and K. D. Williams, "Social Loafing: A Meta-Analytic Review and Theoretical Integration," *Journal of Personality and Social Psychology* 65 (1993): 681–706.

7. For more detailed descriptions and examples of these pathologies, see Merchant and Pick, *Blind Spots, Biases and Other Pathologies.* Our primary concern in

this chapter is to consider ways in which board leaders and board members can take steps to minimize the occurrence and the effects of these boardroom pathologies.

8. C. K. W. De Dreu and L. R. Weingart, "Task Versus Relationship Conflict, Team Performance, Team Member Satisfaction: A Meta-analysis," *Journal of Applied Psychology* 88 (2004): 741–749.

9. Nemeth, "Differential Contributions."

10. D. W. Hock, *Birth of the Chaordic Age* (San Francisco: Berrett-Koehler, 1999).

# Seven

# The Argument for a Separate Chair

DAVID A. NADLER

The question of board leadership is back in the news, despite the fact that only about one-fifth of Standard & Poor's (S&P) 1500 companies have a separate and independent chairman of the board distinct from the CEO.[1] This call for change has been gaining traction. In the wake of the financial and economic crisis of 2008–2009, various interest groups have become more insistent that companies separate the roles of CEO and chairman. Organizations that rate the quality of public company governance give higher grades to companies that separate the positions. In 2009, the Millstein Center for Corporate Governance and Performance at Yale issued a policy briefing in support of the nonexecutive chairman role.[2] More important, the Dodd-Frank bill requires companies to disclose publically their board leadership structure (combined or separate CEO and chairman) and explain the reasons why that structure was chosen.[3]

In light of this renewed interest, it seemed time for me to revisit the subject. In 2004, along with Jay Lorsch, I chaired a blue ribbon commission chartered by the National Association of Corporate Directors (NACD) to examine this very issue. The group included directors, executives, academics, advocates, and advisers representing a range of positions on the corporate governance spectrum. Over a period of almost six months, the more than fifty members of this specially assembled commission were interviewed and surveyed, and then participated in a full-day working session in Washington, DC. The commission debated different aspects of board leadership and published a report in the fall of 2004 that presented the following conclusion:

> Based on the views of the majority of the Commissioners, the research to date, and our own experiences, we believe that separation of the chair and CEO roles is not a requirement for effective board leadership. In fact, while this arrangement may work in some situations, there is no research support for the argument that the separation of roles, in and of itself, creates more effective governance. On the other hand, we do believe that there is a need for leadership to focus the work of the independent directors. So, where the chair and CEO roles are not separated, we believe that there should be a designated leadership role for an independent director to serve as a focal point for the work of all the independent directors, with clarity of role and continuity of who performs that role.[4]

The report supported the idea of independent board leadership, but it was a bit of a soft recommendation: it talked about the position serving as "a focal point for the work of all the independent directors." At the time, there was some discussion in the commission about whether that meant an independent leader of the board or just a leader of the independent directors within the board. Currently, U.S. company boards have reached the point at which they have an average of only 1.2 nonindependent directors, so that issue has become moot. However, we were clear back in 2004 that we were not recommending one structure over another.

In the period since the commission, there has been an ongoing debate and emerging research on this topic. Moreover, along with my consulting colleagues at Oliver Wyman, I have been immersed in board activity in various roles, including consultant, researcher, member of senior management, and board member. I have personally studied and participated in a variety of board leadership models. Based on my experience and observation over the past six years, I have concluded that the time has come for true independent board leadership and that the most effective way to implement such leadership is through the creation of an independent nonexecutive chairman of the board. However, for this approach to succeed, it requires not only the right structure (separation of the roles) but also the right people and the right process.

## The Need for Independent Board Leadership

I remain deeply committed, as I was in 2004, to the crucial need for independent board leadership; if anything, I feel even more strongly about it now. Governance has evolved in the United States, and boards have become more independent and more empowered. Over the long term, the average tenure of CEOs continues to decrease,[5] which makes it more than likely that a board will be forced to replace the CEO before his or her normal term of office is concluded.

Why is there a need for independent leadership? The fundamental impetus has been the change that occurred over the past decade in the de facto hierarchical relationship between the board and the CEO. Before then, the governance system in corporate America was such that the board essentially worked for the CEO. CEOs frequently talked about "my board" in a proprietary sense. Boards were populated by internal directors who reported to the CEO and to external directors who were chosen by the CEO, served at the pleasure of the CEO, were frequently friends or colleagues of the CEO, and often had reciprocal board memberships. In this environment, the board was basically an assemblage of friends, employees, and business associates who acted primarily as compliant advisers to the all-powerful CEO. There's a reason the term "imperial CEO" became so common: it was accurate.

The situation began to change in the early 1990s, when more than two dozen boards of major American companies acted to dismiss their CEOs. This marked a potential watershed in governance, but the subsequent economic boom resulted in a resurgence of the imperial CEO model. It was not until the dot.com bust and the scandals at the turn of the century that momentum for governance reform resumed, powered by the Sarbanes-Oxley legislation and the New York Stock Exchange's new listing requirements. In the years that followed, the relationship between the board and the CEO changed dramatically. At some companies, the CEO began to see the board as his or her "boss." The board became more active in a number of areas, including the evaluation and selection of the CEO, executive compensation, and the selection of directors.

This transformation of the board's role and its relationship to the CEO created a new problem I've described as "circularity" (figure 7-1). In the combined chairman/CEO model, the CEO functions as the leader or "boss" of the board. In this role, he or she leads the board in its work, determining the agenda, chairing meetings, assigning work to directors (individually or through committees), and giving directors feedback on their performance. Yet in this new environment, the board also functions as the CEO's supervisor: it conducts an annual performance evaluation, determines the CEO's compensation, oversees the succession process (including decisions about when to replace the CEO), and is responsible for reviewing and approving or rejecting major proposals brought to the board by the CEO.

The result is an inherently circular situation, rife with confused roles and potential conflicts of interest. How can a CEO who sees the board as his or her "boss" serve as the boss of that very same board? The answer we arrived at in 2004 was that someone other than the CEO—an independent director—had to assume the CEO's function as leader of the board.

FIGURE 7-1

## The circularity problem

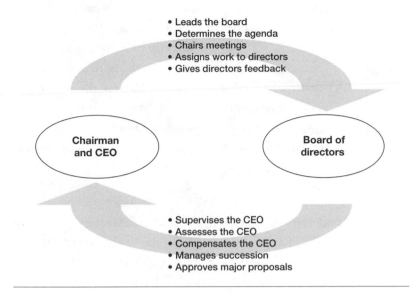

- Leads the board
- Determines the agenda
- Chairs meetings
- Assigns work to directors
- Gives directors feedback

**Chairman and CEO**

**Board of directors**

- Supervises the CEO
- Assesses the CEO
- Compensates the CEO
- Manages succession
- Approves major proposals

As outgrowths of the circularity issue, there are other compelling reasons to structure independent board leadership:

- *Managing the Work of the Board.* With changes in corporate governance, the board now has real work to do, and that work has to be managed. There is a need to establish the agenda, maintain a timely flow of useful information, and ensure that committees are doing their jobs. Separating the chairman and CEO roles creates a job specifically dedicated to managing the board's work while removing the CEO from the untenable position of trying to supervise the group for which he or she works.

- *Managing the Performance of Individual directors.* The new governance environment imposes an unprecedented obligation on directors to perform their roles professionally and diligently, rather than as members of a social club. That means not only showing up—something that couldn't always be taken for granted in the past—but coming prepared and participating actively. When a director's performance falls short, someone needs to provide him or her with feedback, guidance, and even coaching. Again, there's an inherent problem with expecting the CEO to provide tough feedback and rigorous coaching to a director who will directly influence the CEO's own performance evaluation and compensation. Moreover, the independent board leader is able to observe the behavior of directors in those situations in which the CEO would not be present, such as executive sessions and meetings of independent directors in committees (compensation, audit, nominating and governance, etc.).

- *Creating a Sounding Board for the CEO.* The independent board leader provides the CEO with a resource for testing ideas—for determining what matters need to come to the board, and when and how to bring them. This enables the CEO to stay connected without having to deal with the full board in a formal session or, alternatively, communicate with each of the independent directors through multiple interactions.

- *Building an Early Warning System.* The independent leader can also provide the CEO with an early warning when something might be going off track. It could be a situation with an individual director that needs to be addressed or a matter that is emerging in the board as a whole but is not yet visible to the CEO. The independent leader can help the CEO to recognize these concerns early on and assist in formulating the appropriate response.

- *Enabling the Board to Act Independently When Needed.* The independent leader has the capacity to organize the board to take action, particularly in those instances where the issue involves the CEO. These could range from health problems to legal circumstances that essentially make it impossible for the CEO to play a leading, or even active, role. A formal independent leadership structure provides a routine process for engaging the board in the CEO's absence.

Assuming that there is a case for independent board leadership, precisely what does the term signify? In our 2004 work, we articulated three possible board leadership roles, and these still seem like relevant possibilities. Table 7-1 (based on the NACD Blue Ribbon Commission report) outlines the areas of responsibility for each of these roles. First, it defines the role traditionally assumed by the combined chair/CEO. Then it describes the roles that were viewed as two alternate approaches to independent leadership—the nonexecutive chair and the lead independent director. In light of subsequent experiences and observations, however, each of these options needs to be considered in a new light.

TABLE 7-1

## Board leadership roles

| | Chair/CEO model | | Nonexecutive chair model |
|---|---|---|---|
| Areas of responsibility | Chair/CEO role | Lead director role | Nonexecutive chair role |
| Full board meetings | Has the authority to call meetings of the board of directors.<br><br>Chairs meetings of the board of directors and the annual meeting of shareholders. | Participates in board meetings like every other director.<br><br>Acts as intermediary—at times, the chair may refer to the lead director for guidance or to have something taken up in executive session.<br><br>Suggests calling full board meetings to the chair when appropriate. | Has the authority to call meetings of the board of directors.<br><br>Chairs meetings of the board of directors and the annual meeting of shareholders. |

(continued)

TABLE 7-1 (Continued)

## Board leadership roles

| Areas of responsibility | Chair/CEO model | | Nonexecutive chair model |
| --- | --- | --- | --- |
| | Chair/CEO role | Lead director role | Nonexecutive chair role |
| Executive sessions | Receives feedback from the executive sessions. | Has the authority to call meetings of the independent directors.<br><br>Sets the agenda for and leads executive sessions of the independent directors.<br><br>Briefs the CEO on issues arising in the executive sessions. | Has the authority to call meetings of the independent directors.<br><br>Sets the agenda for and leads executive sessions of the independent directors.<br><br>Briefs the CEO on issues arising in the executive sessions. |
| Board agendas and information | Takes primary responsibility for shaping board agendas, consulting with the lead director to ensure that board agendas and information provide the board with what is needed to fulfill its primary responsibilities. | Collaborates with the chair/CEO to set the board agenda and board information.<br><br>Seeks agenda input from other directors. | Takes primary responsibility for shaping board agendas in collaboration with the CEO; consults with all directors to ensure that board agendas and information provide the board with what is needed to fulfill its primary responsibilities. |
| Board communications | Communicates with all directors on key issues and concerns outside of board meetings. | Facilitates discussion among the independent directors on key issues and concerns outside of board meetings.<br><br>Serves as a nonexclusive conduit (to the CEO) of views, concerns, and issues of the independent directors. | Facilitates discussion among the independent directors on key issues and concerns outside of board meetings.<br><br>Serves as a nonexclusive conduit (to the CEO) of views, concerns, and issues of the independent directors. |

TABLE 7-1 (Continued)

## Board leadership roles

| Areas of responsibility | Chair/CEO model | | Nonexecutive chair model |
|---|---|---|---|
| | Chair/CEO role | Lead director role | Nonexecutive chair role |
| External stake-holders | Represents the organization to and interacts with external stakeholders and employees. | Typically has no role in representing the organization to external stake-holders. Some boards, however, occasionally ask their lead director to participate in meetings with key institutional investors. | Can represent the organiza-tion to and interact with external stakeholders and employees at the discretion of the board of directors. |
| Company operations | Leads company operations.<br><br>Officers/ employees report to him or her. | Has no role in company operations.<br><br>Officers/ employees report to CEO, not to him or her. | Has no role in company operations.<br><br>Officers/employees report to CEO, not to him or her. |

*Source*: National Association of Corporate Directors, *Report of the NACD Blue Ribbon Commission on Board Leadership* (Washington, DC: 2004).

## The Nonexecutive Chair

The simplest and most effective way to provide for independent leadership of the board is to bifurcate the leadership role into a CEO position and a nonexecutive chairman of the board position. The nonexecutive chairman (this position and person will be referred to as "the chair"), though, needs to be truly independent to meet the independence guidelines of Sarbanes-Oxley, which means that CEOs who move into the chair position upon retirement would not be considered legitimate independent leaders of the board. In fact, although recent reports indicate that approximately 40 percent of major U.S. companies have separate chairman and CEO roles, more than half of these have a chairman who is an insider/employee or an affiliated outsider.[6] In 2010, only 19 percent of the boards of the S&P 500 reported having board chairs who were truly independent.[7]

## Advantages

The nonexecutive chair provides all the benefits of independent leadership discussed previously, plus some additional advantages:

- *Increased Clarity of Board Leadership.* Creation of the nonexecutive chair position clarifies who runs the board—specifically, who runs the meetings, manages the work processes, and deals with director performance issues. It eliminates some of the potential ambiguity surrounding board leadership when there is a lead director and an executive chairman of the board.

- *Greater Capacity for External Representation.* As chair, the independent board leader has more legitimacy in handling external issues. As such, this individual can assist the CEO and speak for the corporation in dealings with regulators, external advocates, or other constituencies.

- *Greater Credibility for Internal Communication.* The nonexecutive chair also has clear legitimacy in dealing with internal constituencies. At times, it may be useful for the management or employees to hear from the board, and the chair has indisputable credibility in speaking for the board. At one company going through a period of major crisis, many in management began to question the effectiveness of the CEO. At a senior management off-site meeting, the chairman of the board showed up and provided a perspective on the company and the challenges it faced. Following his appearance, many members of management said they felt tremendously reassured that the board of directors understood the issues and that there was responsible leadership of the board.

- *Easier Transition of Authority in the Case of a Disabled CEO.* If the CEO is disabled, the nonexecutive chair can easily step forward and fill the gap. This can be true even in temporary situations. One CEO, for instance, was unable to attend the annual shareholders meeting because of a death in his family. Nonetheless, the meeting was held as scheduled, since it was natural for the chairman to convene and chair it.

- *Greater Durability.* The nonexecutive chair is a formal role within the company's governance structure. By comparison, the lead director role is less visible to the outside world (although disclosure of the leadership structure is now required). I observed a CEO who had encouraged his board to create a lead director role, but when the director filling that role retired, the CEO retreated to a more passive model of rotating presiding directors. This change was not noted by any external observers of the firm and was the subject of little discussion by the board itself. Subsequently, when the company ran into major problems, the board panicked and summarily removed the CEO. Those close to the company commented that this would not have happened had the previous lead director still been an active participant in the board. Even more so, had this board created a nonexecutive chair position, any effort to do away with this position (and thus name the CEO chairman as well) would likely have garnered much attention and been resisted. The explicit formality of the nonexecutive chair structure gives it more stability and makes it more difficult to move in and out of the structure by going under the radar.

## Potential Issues

Although the nonexecutive chair role has a number of significant advantages, it may also give rise to certain problems.

The greatest risk is that the nonexecutive chair can become such a dominating figure that he or she disempowers the CEO. The chair becomes the de facto CEO, undermining the effectiveness of the actual CEO and defeating the entire purpose of independent leadership. In such extreme cases, the chair loses the distance required to objectively evaluate how well the company is being managed.

A dominating chair can also disempower other directors. The chair can interfere with the communication between directors and the CEO by functioning as an exclusive conduit for board communication. He or she can also be so dominant at board and committee meetings that the other directors do not have an opportunity for meaningful input and participation.

Another risk is micromanagement or inappropriate intervention by the chair. When that happens, the chair does not dominate the CEO, but he or she does get improperly involved in the day-to-day management of the company. For example, one chair took it upon himself to provide key officers of the company with feedback on their performance and behavior without consulting the CEO. This confused the executives because the chair's input, based on a very limited view of their overall performance, conflicted with the feedback they received from their boss, the CEO.

To be sure, there are times when the CEO and the chair can come into conflict, and that's not necessarily a bad thing; constructive contention can lead to better decisions. The problem is when the conflict becomes public, raising questions about the direction of the corporation and politicizing the decision-making process within the company. This occurred in the early days of the post-bankruptcy General Motors restructuring, when the chair was openly critical of the GM management. Similar problems arose at AIG in 2010 between the CEO and the chair. When the two are at odds in a public way, what are executives to do?

At the other extreme, the nonexecutive chair role can fail if the individual in that role does not take enough initiative, provide enough leadership, or act with enough independence to gain the advantages that should accrue from the role.

The structure at the top—whether separate or combined CEO and chair positions—is an important enabler of independent board leadership, but ultimately, its success depends on how the roles are enacted. As with other aspects of board functioning, it is the

TABLE 7-2

**Preconditions for an effective independent chair structure**

| Characteristics of the individual | Characteristics of the process |
| --- | --- |
| Business acumen | Role clarity |
| Credibility | Maintenance of director–CEO relationships |
| Interpersonal skills | Effective collaboration |
| Leadership skills | Broad director participation |
| Appropriate motivation | Appropriate selection approach |
| Compatibility with the CEO | Complementary in-board leadership |

dynamics, rather than the mechanics, that are more important. It is the actions of various individuals, but particularly of the two people in the CEO and chair roles (their behavior, their relationship, their self-awareness), that determine whether the structure operates in a way that yields the desired benefits, or whether it fails or even produces unintended negative consequences. In the end, it is imperative both to select the right person to fill the chair role and to build the right kinds of behavioral and work processes (table 7-2).

## Picking the Right Person

What kind of person is best for the chair role? To state the obvious, the requirements differ depending on the industry, the company, and the current condition of the company. Looking across a variety of boards, however, it appears that the best chairs share the following characteristics:

- *Business Acumen.* In order to serve as a true partner to the CEO, the chair needs to bring a broad understanding of business and how business organizations function. Ideally, such knowledge should span a variety of industries and companies; it usually comes from a range of business experiences and, in particular, senior management experience. This enables the chair to appreciate the challenges that face the CEO and his or her team and also to recognize how the board can help or hinder CEO and executive team performance. Business acumen is critical for establishing a balance of knowledge and power between the chair and the CEO and other directors.

- *Credibility.* A related characteristic is the credibility of the individual. This is important because it bestows the power to lead—in relation to the CEO, in relation to the other directors, and in relation to various external and internal constituencies. Credibility can stem from business acumen, but it is also a product of certain unique aspects of individuals— their life experiences, how they conduct themselves, how well they communicate, their perceived ethics, their gravitas, and their proven knowledge of the issues that the board faces.

- *Interpersonal Skills.* The chair role requires expertise at managing in a network of complex and dynamic interpersonal relations, including the relationship with the CEO, intraboard relationships, board–management relationships, and, potentially, relationships with external actors. The chair must be able to build effective connections, possess sufficient emotional intelligence to sense how he or she is affecting others, and have the capacity to collaborate. The relationship with the CEO, in particular, is inherently one of partnership. The person who leads the company and the person who leads the board must find ways to collaborate so that they provide clear leadership through their joint efforts. That doesn't mean they will always agree; it does mean they will find a constructive way to work through their inevitable differences. And that requires strong interpersonal skills.

- *Leadership Skills.* Another factor, which is implicit but sometimes not considered, relates to the group leadership skills of the individual. While the relationship with the CEO is important, the relationship with other members of the board is equally critical. Given that the board is essentially a team of peers, the leadership approach needs to be inclusive and take advantage of the resources and competencies in the team. Capable team leaders know how to structure the work, how to engage people in the work process, and how to move them toward a decision. Those who have led in a classic command-and-control style may be less effective in this type of environment. The nature of the board role and composition requires a more facilitative approach to leadership, with a sensitivity to group dynamics.

- *Appropriate Motivation.* Another aspect that is fundamental but harder to assess is the psychological state of the individual who might become chair—specifically, what motivates him or her to take on the role. The risk here involves frustrated would-be CEOs who have unmet needs for power or recognition and see the role of chair as a way to satisfy these needs. Such individuals are more likely to engage in micromanaging or to dominate the CEO. On the other hand, we have observed people in the chair role who were reluctant nominees and adopted a passive stance, thus creating a leadership vacuum.

- *Compatibility with the CEO.* Ultimately, these situations work best when the chair and the CEO are compatible in terms of their personal characteristics, motivations, styles, and psychological state. Some combinations can be especially advantageous, whereas others are problematic. At one company I've worked with closely, I watched the chair and the president/CEO, over a period of three years, build a relationship that functioned effectively. The chair brought business acumen, credibility, experience as a former CEO, experience on other boards, and significant motivation to do the job well. The CEO, previously a very successful chairman and CEO at another firm, was secure in his leadership capabilities and comfortable with the split roles. In the end, it was precisely this compatibility that helped to make the structure so effectual.

# The Right Process

One can have the right structure and the right individual to fill the role of chair, but still fail to create an effective leadership team for the corporation. The final factor is how the leadership structure is implemented—the ways of working together, the types of relationships, and the patterns of behavior. Following are some keys to success:

- *Role Clarity.* It is important to establish clear roles and determine what is to be done by the CEO and what is to be done by the chair. Clarity of roles helps to avoid a collision between two designated leaders of the corporation (one of the company and one of the board). It is also important to clarify the role of chair as contrasted to the roles of the other directors, including the roles of key committee chairs. In all of this, it is essential to specify that the chair is leading the board, not leading the company.

- *Maintenance of Director–CEO Relationships.* As the role of chair is enacted, it is critical to maintain the relationship between the CEO and the other independent directors. The CEO needs to have direct access to the other directors—for advice, for assistance, or to help in working on board issues. There is enough work to be done that one should avoid funneling every transaction through the chair. At the same time, individual directors need to feel that as shareholder representatives with fiduciary duties, they have direct access to the CEO.

- *Effective Collaboration.* As mentioned earlier, the two leaders must work together as a kind of team to provide the requisite leadership for the entire institution. Having the right individuals is necessary but not sufficient. They must demonstrate that they can work together productively, which requires building a positive, collaborative relationship. Collaboration implies the ability to share views, combine knowledge and experience, solve problems together, and support each other.

It also signifies the ability to surface and deal with divergent views and even outright conflict.

- *Broad Director Participation.* If the board is a team of individuals who need to work together,[8] then the process of working with the chair should facilitate broad, constructive participation by all board members.

- *Appropriate Selection Approach.* Given all the elements involved in getting the right person, it is critical to define an appropriate process for selecting the chair. Officially, the chair should be elected by the directors, and it normally falls to the nominating and governance committee of the board to propose candidates. This can be complicated, however, by the fact that the chair may serve on that committee. Therefore, a clear process for selection—one that takes this possibility into consideration—must be determined ahead of time. In addition, as with any key leader, there needs to be agreement about how the chair will get feedback on his or her performance, and (in the extreme) about the process by which the board can remove and replace the chair.

- *Complementary In-board Leadership.* Sometimes it becomes useful for the board to identify an internal counterpoint to a powerful and active chair. Because the chair is the de facto manager of the CEO, it can be difficult for the CEO to provide balance if the chair becomes too dominant or is determined to micromanage. In those instances, another independent director (in some cases, the chair of the nominating and governance committee) can serve as that counterbalance, taking it upon himself or herself to provide the chair with feedback and guidance. This can also come from any individual director who has the necessary credibility and is able to provide constructive input.

My conclusion is that if the board is able to find the right person and build the right process, the nonexecutive chair role can be a very valuable and effective mechanism. If that is the case, then why would boards consider any other approach?

# The Lead Independent Director

In the early 1990s, as the first rumblings of board independence and empowerment were being heard, Jay Lorsch and Marty Lipton proposed the idea of creating a new job—the lead independent director.[9] In doing so, they identified an alternative structure—one that created independent leadership but stopped short of splitting the CEO and chair roles.

As demonstrated in table 7-1, the lead independent director ("lead director") position was seen as having many of the same features as the nonexecutive chair, but with a different title and a somewhat diminished set of responsibilities. What are the advantages of the lead director structure? Basically, it is a means to achieve the benefits of separating board leadership while maintaining the clarity of unitary corporate leadership. It avoids ambiguity about who is in charge of the corporation, and therefore avoids some of the potential downsides of the nonexecutive chair role. It has proven to be an effective model that does not require a structural change at the top.

A notable example of this model exists at Tyco International. In the aftermath of the corporate irregularities and scandals during the term of CEO Dennis Kozlowski, Tyco searched for a new CEO. The candidate who emerged was Ed Breen, a senior executive at Motorola and former CEO of General Instruments. Breen took the position on the condition that he could build a new board of directors. He began by recruiting retired DuPont CEO Jack Krol as lead director, who in turn recruited other directors to the new board. Over a period of close to seven years, Krol and Breen built a very productive partnership: Krol provided active leadership for the board, while Breen led the company.

At the same time, there are some potential disadvantages to the lead director approach:

- A lead director structure still leaves some ambiguity about board leadership. Who is leading the board? There is a chairman of the board, but there is another individual who leads the board in certain areas and at certain times. It begs the question of whether the circularity problem is really being resolved.

- The lead director has less stature and legitimacy to function externally. He or she is not necessarily in a position to represent the company.

- The lead director is inherently an informal position, and therefore can be more easily modified (as mentioned earlier).

- The lead director role can still run into many of the same problems as the nonexecutive chair in terms of individuals who are dominating or who interfere with managers.

So what is important for the success of this approach? The issues are comparable to those with the nonexecutive chair. The right person needs to be selected, and the appropriate interpersonal and work processes need to be instituted and managed. For this to happen, the role must be established explicitly and managed in such a way that there is clarity about the selection process and continuity of leadership, with no easy escape hatch to permit disabling the role.

On reflection, the lead director structure can provide some of the elements of independent leadership, but it has no clear advantages over the nonexecutive chair except that it does not necessitate an obvious structural change at the top that comes from the formal separation of the CEO and chairman roles. The question then is, Why haven't more boards moved toward the nonexecutive chair model? There are three basic reasons: resistance from CEOs to giving up the chairman title, the challenge of having to deal with another potentially powerful actor in the boardroom, and concern about the signals that inadvertently might be sent by the change.

Certainly, there are other possible explanations. In some cases, it has been difficult to find the right individual to serve as chair (although lately there has been a trend toward bringing in people directly as chairs, rather than selecting a chair from among existing directors).[10] Another explanation is that boards are hesitant to make the move because it might be interpreted as a negative reflection on the current CEO. In fact, a number of very visible efforts to separate the chair/CEO structure (e.g., Disney, Bank of America) have been seen as an unfavorable message from the board about the CEO and have in fact preceded the CEO's departure. Some boards have considered changing the structure when a new CEO is appointed, but have wondered whether it would be interpreted as tepid or less-than-wholehearted support of the incoming CEO.

## My Recommendation

The shape of corporate governance in the United States is fluid; we are in the midst of a historic transition, and the pace of change is accelerating. Approaches that seemed reasonable ten years ago—or even as recently as 2004—must be reexamined in the light of growing demands for transparent, independent, and responsible governance. Today, given the evolution of governance in this country and in the interest of sustaining governance of the highest quality, I recommend that boards formally designate a nonexecutive chairman. In my opinion, other things being equal, the nonexecutive chair should be regarded as the superior structure because it provides more clarity of board leadership and offers more advantages. I do not see lead directors or having a recently retired CEO serving as chairman to be fulfilling the intent of independent leadership.

One potential counterargument is that the right candidate does not exist in the board, but this applies to the lead director role as well. Thus, all that remains is concern about the signals that are being sent regarding the incumbent or incoming CEO, and those can be managed. To avoid sending unintended messages about the quality of leadership, boards should openly adopt the new structure, to be implemented upon the next CEO succession. In this way, the change would not be interpreted as a statement about the current or incoming CEO.

Then, once a board chooses to elect a nonexecutive chair, the first critical step is the selection of this independent leader. A vital factor is picking the right person for the role. The implication is that the nominating and governance committee needs to be thinking about the leadership pipeline and leadership development within the board as much as they think about these issues within the company. As directors are recruited, the committee and the board need to consider whether they are bringing in people with the requisite skills to serve in the leadership role. Given that directors often have other obligations that might keep them from serving as chair, boards would do well to have a surplus of eligible talent. Having brought in the talent, the committee then must decide how to develop individuals so that they have the experience, exposure, and relationships in the board and with management to function in a board leadership role. The alternative is to go outside and select a new director who could immediately serve as chair; however, there are risks associated with this approach, much as with any outside senior-level hire.

Also, after this leadership structure has been enacted, designing and maintaining the leadership process is essential because effective board leadership is the result of the right structure combined with the right people and the right interpersonal and work processes. Structure is important, but less so than the individuals who are in the roles and how they enact those roles and relationships. Everyone involved has to pay attention to designing the right processes and making sure that the processes evolve effectively over time.

It is also important to note that, despite the clear advantages of the nonexecutive chair role, boards must remain flexible and recognize that when it comes to governance structures, one size does not fit all. Different companies and boards face different challenges in different contexts. They also have different human capital on which to draw. Although I urge boards to move toward the nonexecutive chair structure, I do not support legislation that would mandate it, nor do I support governance ratings that necessarily give higher scores or grades to boards that separate the chairman and CEO roles. Such approaches focus exclusively on structure and ignore the issues of people and process.

In summary, the time has come for true independent leadership. Each and every board needs to ensure that it has such leadership—that it has the right structure, the right people, and the right process. Over time, boards would be acting in the best interests of their shareholders by migrating toward separate chairman and CEO roles.

## Notes

1. Millstein Center for Corporate Governance and Performance, Yale School of Management, "Prevalence of Board Leadership Structures," 2009, http://millstein.som.yale.edu/chairmensforum.shtml.

2. Millstein Center for Corporate Governance and Performance, Yale School of Management, *Chairing the Board: The Case for Independent Leadership in Corporate North America*, policy briefing no. 4 (New Haven, CT: Author, 2009).

3. U.S. Congress, *Dodd-Frank Wall Street Reform and Consumer Protection Act*, HR 4173, Section 972.

4. National Association of Corporate Directors, *Report of the NACD Blue Ribbon Commission on Board Leadership* (Washington, DC: Author, 2004).

5. K. Favaro, P. Karlsson, and G. L. Neilson, "CEO Succession 2000–2009: A Decade of Convergence and Compression," *Strategy + Business* 59 (2010): 76–91.

6. Millstein Center for Corporate Governance and Performance, *Prevalence of Board Leadership Structures*.

7. Spencer Stuart, *Spencer Stuart Board Index* (New York: Author, 2010).

8. D. A. Nadler, B. A. Behan, and M. B. Nadler, eds., *Building Better Boards: A Blueprint for Effective Governance* (San Francisco: Jossey-Bass, 2006).

9. M. Lipton and J. Lorsch, "A Modest Proposal for Improved Corporate Governance," *The Business Lawyer* 48 (1992): 59–76.

10. J. Lublin, "Ex-CEOs lend Struggling Companies a Hand." *The Wall Street Journal*, November 9, 2009.

# Eight

# The Argument for a Lead Director

RAYMOND GILMARTIN

As a retired chairman and CEO, I was very wary of the idea of a lead or presiding director. It was difficult for me to understand why a chairman and CEO, like I had been, could not lead the board. I began to understand, however, that as independent directors became more active and influential in major companies, it was important for them to have a leader who was not also the CEO. On the boards on which I was serving, the directors were not in favor of separating the roles of chairman and CEO. Instead, they opted for a lead or presiding director (I soon came to realize that the two titles were interchangeable). Then, when I found myself selected to this position on the boards of two major companies, my interest in the role's potential and importance was heightened.

I soon realized that the core of the job was to serve as a leader among the independent directors and as a liaison between them and the CEO. I also became highly aware of the distinction between this role and that of the separate chairman, which is prevalent in many places outside the United States, because the lead director remains an equal with the other directors, not their boss, which so many chairmen consider themselves to be. After some years acting as a lead director and a presiding director, I have come to believe that a lead or presiding director can be a more effective leader than a separate chairman because the lead director can perform similar duties to a separate chairman without becoming a second power center on the board who has the potential to dominate not only the CEO but also the other directors.

## The Need for Independent Board Leadership

In the 1970s, the subject of corporate governance acquired increasing importance.[1] "[T]his attention emanated from groups and interests which for one reason or another were dissatisfied with some aspect of corporate behavior and which sought to reform the structure and process of corporate governance."[2] These parties included business leaders, regulators, academics, social reformers, consumer advocates, religious groups, unions, and environmentalists.[3]

These critics were convinced that boards were not fully equipped to oversee management. According to their critique, boards were too often composed of members of management or individuals who shared close relationships with the CEO. The meetings themselves were filled with formal presentations rather than fruitful discussion and debate. As a result, those pressing for change thought that "the norms of polite boardroom behavior discouraged directors from openly questioning or challenging the CEO's performance or proposals."[4]

They also believed that there would be serious repercussions if directors did not rectify these dynamics in the boardroom. As a prominent academic said at the time, "Numerous community leaders [were] persuaded that revitalization of the board of directors was urgently needed to assure the continued development of the large organizations as a constructive influence in contemporary society."[5] In 1974, Ray Garrett, the then chairman of the Securities and Exchange Commission, said in a speech:

> The agency is working toward a reasonable director concept. The typical, well-orchestrated board meeting, with the quick agenda, followed by some report of general interest on the operation of the business, followed by lunch, all on a tight schedule, induces an atmosphere of compliance and non-inquiry that may be dangerous.[6]

Because of such pressure, boards began to reevaluate their composition, responsibilities, and purpose; by the 1980s, they were becoming more assertive and independent. Also by that time, approximately 70 percent of all corporate directors were independent,[7] thus creating a "better balance of boardroom power."[8]

## An Emerging Concept: The Lead Director

In 1989, Jay Lorsch published a comprehensive study on the subject of corporate boards.[9] He prescribed various reforms to improve directors' ability to govern. Among these changes, he recommended that boards elect a presiding director to serve as the board's leader during times of crisis. According to Lorsch, the initial idea was that "the presiding director would have no duties until the CEO was incapacitated or a majority of the outside directors felt the need for new board leadership."[10] Although this proposal only applied to crisis periods, Lorsch was the first to recommend a structural change that would afford independent directors "greater power."[11]

Shortly thereafter, in 1992, Lorsch teamed up with Marty Lipton and coined the term *lead director*. According to their article published in *The Business Lawyer*, a lead director would act in both normal times and crises and would convey the concerns of the independent directors to management, help set the board agendas, manage crisis situations involving the CEO or senior management or both, and assist with the selection of board committee members. This was a more prominent role than what Lorsch himself had proposed a few years prior. They believed that "independent directors needed some form of leadership among their own if they were to be effective,"[12] and according to Lorsch, "we thought that boards would resist separating the roles of chairman and CEO so this was, in our view, the next best option."[13]

## Brewing Change

However, despite these arguments, the lead director concept was not adopted by many boards during the 1990s. In addition, the public continued to voice grievances about independent directors' inability to counteract the influence of management. The General Motors board was a prime example of such board failure that caused public alarm. In this case, the GM board did not make timely decisions, which caused the company to nearly collapse in 1992.[14] However, after being advised by Ira Millstein,[15] who was also an advocate of implementing leadership of the independent directors, the board finally stepped in and removed its underperforming CEO, Robert Stempel. The GM board also decided to separate the roles of chairman and CEO. Jack Smith succeeded Stempel as CEO, and John Smale, the former CEO of Procter & Gamble, became the chairman. A few years later, in 1995, the board seemed to reverse itself, giving Smith the titles of both chairman and CEO and naming Smale lead director.[16]

In the minds of many, the decisions by the GM board were a retreat from best-practice corporate governance because separating the roles of chairman and CEO was still believed to be the most effective way to establish independent board leadership. The situation at GM demonstrated that, in the minds of many, the separate chairman remained a more highly regarded leader in comparison with a lead director.

### Corporate Scandals

The corporate governance landscape changed significantly following the scandals of 2001 and 2002, including Enron, WorldCom, and Tyco. "In the wake of these multibillion-dollar financial debacles, a public distrust of management and board insiders [erupted]."[17] As a result, the Sarbanes-Oxley Act (SOX) was passed in 2002. The act mandated that audit committees consist entirely of independent directors, maintain at least one financial expert, and retain and oversee the company's independent auditor.

Then, the major stock exchanges (the New York Stock Exchange [NYSE] and NASDAQ) issued new corporate governance listing standards in 2004, two years after the guidelines were first proposed (table 8-1). According to these standards, the majority of directors were required to be independent and hold routine executive sessions without management present. The NYSE mandated that the executive sessions be led by a "presiding director," whereas NASDAQ did not specify the need for such a position. The Sarbanes-Oxley Act and the listing requirements codified the ongoing trend toward greater board independence.

Boards were confronted with how to respond to the new requirements—some boards were already in compliance, whereas others had to alter their governing structures. Unsurprisingly, these externally imposed changes were met with some resistance.

For example, as Lorsch and Lipton had previously predicted, "some top managers reacted negatively to the idea of a lead director for fear that this individual, like a separate Chairman, could attempt to usurp some of the functions of the CEO and/or management team."[18] Also, directors were concerned about how the role would change the dynamics in the boardroom. Would a lead director diminish the stature of the other directors? How would the independent directors interact with the lead director?

In spite of these reservations, the lead director concept began to emerge as a well-defined and accepted leadership structure. The number of boards that adopted the role skyrocketed in the early 2000s, after Congress passed SOX and the stock exchanges deliberated on and then instituted corporate governance listing requirements (figure 8-1).

## Increasing Calls for Change

At this time, more institutional investors, proxy advisory firms, and other influential organizations began to advocate for companies to either separate the roles of chairman and CEO or to appoint a lead

TABLE 8-1

## Abbreviated summary of the stock exchanges' requirements

| NYSE | NASDAQ |
| --- | --- |
| The majority of directors must be independent. | The majority of directors must be independent. |
| The independent directors must hold an executive session without management, and this meeting shall be overseen by a "presiding director." | Independent directors must regularly convene executive sessions of the independent directors (at least twice per year). |
| Companies must communicate in a way by which "interested parties" can contact the independent directors. | Independent directors must approve director nominations. |
| All directors on the nominating/governance, compensation, and audit committees must be independent. | Independent director approval of CEO and executive officer compensation is required. |
| Each member of the audit committee must be "financially literate" or become "financially literate," and at least one member of the committee must have prior experience in accounting or financial management. | All audit committee members must be able to read and understand financial statements at the time of their appointment. |
| Companies must have an internal audit function. | An audit committee must establish procedures for the receipt, retention, and confidential and anonymous treatment of complaints received by the company regarding accounting; the committee has the sole authority to appoint, determine funding for, and oversee the outside auditors. |
| Companies must create and make public a set of corporate governance guidelines and a code of business conduct. | Issuers must adopt a code of conduct for all directors and employees and make it publicly available. |

*Sources:* Womble, Carlyle, Sandridge & Rice, "NYSE Adopts Final Corporate Governance Rules," November 26, 2003, www.wcsr.com/filefolder/sarbanes4.pdf/; and NASDAQ, *NASDAQ Corporate Governance Summary of Rules Changes,* November 2003, http://www.nasdaq.com/about/CorpGovSummary.pdf.

director. They primarily campaigned for the separation of the roles, but found the lead director to be a suitable compromise.

For example, in 2004, the National Association of Corporate Directors (NACD) published the *Report of the Blue Ribbon Commission on Board Leadership* (see also chapter 7), which stated that "[w]here

FIGURE 8-1

**If your chairman is also the CEO, do you have a lead director among the outside directors?**

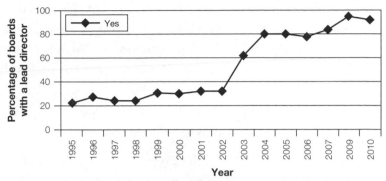

*Note:* Data collected from Korn/Ferry International annual board of directors surveys, 1994 to 2007, and Spencer Stuart, *2010 Spencer Stuart Board Index.*

the chair and CEO roles are not separated, we believe that there should be a designated leadership role for an independent director to serve as a focal point for the work of all the independent directors, with clarity of role and continuity of who performs that role."[19]

Institutional investors advocated for change because they believed that it represented best-practice corporate governance. Although their philosophy had not been proven, institutional investors believed that good corporate governance was correlated with strong performance; therefore, they worked to align companies' governance structures with their model of best practice. By changing the practices within a few companies, they hoped to incite change in others.

The California Public Employee Retirement System (CalPERS), a highly influential institutional investor, published reports on its interpretation of best-practice corporate governance. Its first report was published in the late 1990s. More recently, in its 2010 *Global Principles of Accountable Corporate Governance*, CalPERS stated:

> The board should be chaired by an independent director. The CEO and chair roles should only be combined in limited circumstances; in these situations, the board should provide a written statement in the proxy materials discussing why the

combined role is in the best interest of shareholders, and it should name a lead independent director.[20]

Meanwhile, proxy advisory firms, such as RiskMetrics Group, informed institutional investors on how to vote in board elections and on management proposals. These organizations wielded great influence, and companies paid close attention to the advice that they offered their clients. In RiskMetrics Group's 2010 proxy voting guidelines, it recommended the separation of the roles of chairman and CEO unless the board had appointed a lead director and instituted other structural requirements:

> Generally vote FOR shareholder proposals requiring that the chairman's position be filled by an independent director, unless the company satisfies *all* of the following criteria: [1] Designated lead director, elected by and from the independent board members . . . [,] [2] [t]wo-thirds independent board[,] [3] [a]ll independent key committees[,] [4] [e]stablished governance guidelines[,] [5] . . . must not have exhibited poor total shareholder return performance[, and] [6] [t]he company does not have any problematic governance or management issues.[21]

## Impact of the Financial Crisis

In 2008, the United States experienced what has been labeled the worst financial crisis since the Great Depression. The public and policy makers in Washington believed that boards were asleep at the wheel, which contributed to the severity of the crisis. As a result, the issue of independent board leadership resurfaced, and Congress incorporated guidelines related to board leadership in the 2010 Dodd-Frank Wall Street Reform bill and the Consumer Protection Act.[22]

In large part due to the activists' and Congress's distrust of the business community, the new board leadership rules applied to all public companies, not just financial institutions. According to the legislation, a company was required to disclose, in its proxy statement, the logic behind its board leadership structure. The following is an excerpt from the legislation:

No later than [six months] after the date of enactment of this subsection, the Commission shall issue rules that require an issuer to disclose in the annual proxy sent to investors the reasons why the issuer has chosen—

(1) The same person to serve as chairman of the board of directors and chief executive officer (or in equivalent positions); or

(2) Different individuals to serve as chairman of the board of directors and chief executive officer (or in equivalent positions of the issuer).[23]

This legislation was a validation of the idea born in the 1980s that U.S. directors needed independent leadership of the board. It gave boards a choice—separate the roles of chairman and CEO or elect a lead director. Although the governance activists have continued to push for a separation of the roles, they have now largely accepted either structure. According to a 2010 Spencer Stuart report, 19 percent of boards have a separate chairman, and 92 percent of boards have a lead director.[24] Undoubtedly, there is a growing consensus among directors that a lead director can provide boards with extremely effective leadership without adopting the separate chairman and CEO model.

## The Role and Responsibilities of the Lead Director

*What Do Lead Directors Do?*

There are no guidelines describing the duties of a lead director; as a result, boards can define the role differently. Despite this variability, a lead director is most likely to perform the following duties:

- Develop board agendas with the chairman and CEO

- Advise the chairman and CEO on quality, quantity, and timeliness of information from management

- Act as the principal liaison between the independent directors and the chairman and CEO

- Preside at executive sessions of the independent directors at which the chairman and CEO is not present

- Communicate the discussions that occurred in the executive sessions to the chairman and CEO

- Serve as a spokesperson for the board with management and public

Through these responsibilities, a lead director has the opportunity to add considerable value to the functioning of a board. For example, lead directors have revolutionized boardroom dialogue by presiding over executive sessions of the independent directors. Previously, without executive sessions, the directors and the CEO would too often leave board meetings with a host of unspoken and unresolved issues. A director or a CEO would be wondering, What were the major takeaways from our discussion? What actions should be taken going forward? What were the opinions of the full board versus the opinions of the most vocal directors? The directors and CEO often had difficulty reaching agreements at the end of such board meetings.

However, the executive session has transformed discussions in most boardrooms; not only do the independent directors have a chance to speak openly at the end of meetings, but also the lead director can and does encourage such dialogue in order to synthesize and clarify their opinions (figure 8-2). At these sessions, the lead director serves as a facilitator and helps the directors to reach agreement. He or she creates a safe environment in which the independent directors can talk candidly with one another.

Finally, the lead director relays the concerns and ideas expressed by the independent directors to the CEO. As a lead director and a presiding director myself, I find it beneficial to invite the CEO back into the room after the board finishes with its executive session. This way, the CEO receives feedback when all of the directors are present, and the board is assured that the CEO is presented with an

FIGURE 8-2

**Does the board typically hold regular executive sessions without the CEO?**

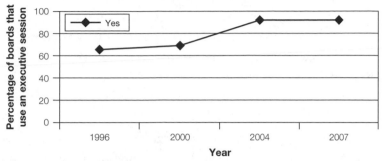

Year

*Note:* Data collected from Korn/Ferry International annual board of directors surveys, 1994 to 2007.

accurate description of its discussion. The directors can add nuances to the lead director's feedback, and the CEO can discern which issues are most important to the full board. The executive session has helped to transform boards from acting as sounding boards to true oversight boards.

These executive sessions have also provided the lead director with a basis to work with the chairman and CEO to develop the board agenda. Based on the conversations that took place at the executive session, the lead director has enough information to represent the board's concerns and therefore influence which issues are addressed at the board meetings. The lead director can also make sure that the chairman and CEO does not dominate the flow of information to influence board discussions and decisions.

## The Expanding Role of the Lead Director

In the last decade, the lead director has taken on "a more complicated portfolio of responsibilities."[25] This is largely because, through their actions, lead directors have gained the confidence of the other directors, who feel comfortable passing more responsibility to them. This trend is reflected in the shift between the use of the two titles of lead and presiding director. When the concept of independent leadership was first introduced, boards were wary of allocating a great deal of responsibility to the lead or presiding director, so they chose the title *presiding*. They believed that this title carried a less authoritative connotation. However, in recent years, the titles have become interchangeable—they both refer to an individual with a high level of responsibility. In 2004, 28 percent of Standard & Poor's 500 boards used *lead director*, whereas 72 percent used *presiding director*. In 2010, 52 percent used *lead director* and 48 percent used *presiding director*.[26]

Also, the members of the Lead Director Network, an organization composed of twenty lead directors, presiding directors, and nonexecutive chairmen from leading U.S. corporations, recently discussed how their titles affect their responsibilities and concluded that "[t]he lead and presiding directors often have essentially the same portfolio of responsibilities. [However], the nonexecutive chairman, in contrast, usually assumes a larger role in company and board leadership."[27]

In addition, some boards had previously chosen to rotate the lead director position among their committee chairs or independent directors on a meeting-by-meeting basis. However, today, only about 5 percent of boards rotate the position. This is further evidence that both the roles of lead and presiding director are considered to be very important.

Finally, the results of a 2010 PricewaterhouseCoopers survey showed this shift as well. The firm surveyed sixty lead directors from U.S. public companies. According to the results, 65 percent believed that their responsibilities would increase in the next two years, 35 percent predicted that they would remain the same, and no one thought that their role would shrink in the next few years.[28]

Based on my conversations with other directors, many believe that they can benefit from the broader involvement of a lead director. Although not all boards have expanded the role, this is the direction in which many boards are heading. The following are some of the areas in which a lead director is likely to gain more responsibility.

## CEO Evaluations and Succession

If the lead director also serves as the chair of the nominating or corporate governance committee, he or she may oversee CEO succession planning activities and the annual CEO evaluation in order to maintain appropriate and effective leadership at the top. On the other hand, it may be difficult for one individual to handle the responsibilities of a lead director and a committee chair, so on many boards the evaluation of the CEO continues to be coordinated by the corporate governance committee.

## Shareholder Communication

In 2004, the NYSE required that all publicly listed companies provide a way for shareholders to contact the independent directors. Therefore, many boards chose to designate the lead director as the "speaker of the board." In my experience, when a lead director engages with shareholders, he or she listens to their concerns and does not attempt to address them at that point in time. Then, after their conversation, the lead director relays this information to both the independent directors and the management team and takes an active role in creating a response plan to address these concerns. Also, a lead director is very conscious of the risk of violating the SEC's Regulation FD (Fair Disclosure). Nonpublic information cannot be disclosed to a shareholder; therefore, the lead director must understand what information is public and nonpublic.

## Major Transactions

Some boards ask the lead director to take a prominent role in the processes and negotiations leading up to major transactions. He or she may advise management, ensure proper due diligence, facilitate discussions among board members, and interact with advisers and shareholders during these critical periods.[29] The role taken by the lead director often depends on a number of factors, including the size of the transaction, the deal structure, and the experience level of management and the board.[30] Additionally, in some cases, a board forms a special committee to oversee and manage this process, and the lead director is almost always a member of this group.[31]

### Crisis Management

Crisis management is also becoming an important responsibility of the lead director. A lead director can manage the board during such critical periods because he or she can provide the independent directors with a credible and independent voice. He or she may mobilize and lead the independent directors during many different crisis situations, such as an acquisition, a change in control, an unsolicited buyout offer, a special investigation, a proxy contest, a sudden resignation of the CEO, or a dysfunctional board.

The members of the Lead Director Network described their roles as "pronounced and intense" during such times. In these cases, the lead director is often one of the first to know about an issue, and if warranted, the lead director presents the situation to the full board. Afterward, the board either decides to form a special committee or addresses the issue through the work of the full board.

### Board Development

Lead directors are beginning to assist with board development. For example, the annual board evaluations, often conducted by the corporate governance or nominating committee, provide directors with information about how the board functions as a group. Traditionally, the chairman or a committee chairman uses these evaluations to pinpoint and address the board's weaknesses. However, a lead director may be in a much better position to respond to the issues that come out of the board evaluation because he or she has in-depth knowledge of the board's thinking.

The lead director can provide clarity regarding how these issues will be addressed by creating concrete action steps. For example, a lead director can maintain a board's focus on the most pressing issues, help the board to arrive at decisions in a timely fashion, deal with the underperformance of a director, ensure that directors receive accurate and timely information from management, and help to forge a productive relationship between the CEO and the board.[32] In addition, a lead director can make a board aware of its deficiencies outside of the annual board evaluations. For example, without a lead director, who is going to acknowledge when a board is ineffectual?

The lead director's role in all of these additional responsibilities remains in its early stages. There are still questions regarding the appropriate role that the lead director should take and the potential for him or her to further contribute to this area without disenfranchising other independent directors.

## Selecting the Lead Director

Based on my observations, a lead director exhibits certain characteristics in order to be successful at his or her role. For example, a lead director should:

- Act as a facilitator

- Be an active listener

- Be able to synthesize discussions of the board and opinions of fellow directors

- Be able to discern which issues the board is most concerned about

- Be able to reach agreement

- Be able to relay the board's concerns to management accurately

These attributes allow a lead director to facilitate agreement and forge common ground among a group of directors with varying perspectives. Also, in my experience, lead directors never express an interest in gaining more power on the board. In fact, I have often thought that the best candidate is not necessarily the most dominant director, and is somebody who does not want the job!

It is extremely important to elect an individual with these traits to serve as the lead director; therefore, some boards are implementing a succession plan for the lead director. When choosing a lead director, it is important to speak with all of the directors, including the chairman and CEO, in order to understand the culture of the board and to hear their recommendations regarding new candidates.[33] Unfortunately, this process does not always occur when selecting a chairman.

## The Alternative Structure: The Nonexecutive Chairman

The choice between board leadership structures is often situational and a reflection of a company's circumstance. For example, a board might choose to elect a separate chairman when transitioning between CEOs, because a separate chairman can work closely with the new CEO and impart institutional knowledge as he or she moves into the new position. However, outside of such special circumstances, boards would do well to keep the roles of CEO and chairman combined, because a separate chairman is liable to set up another power center on the board and within the company.

The chairman is supposed to be the leader of the board; however, he or she often acts like the leader of the company. For example, a separate chairman may set up an office at the company's headquarters, get involved in the operations of the business, cut off communication between the CEO and other board members, or act like a second CEO. This creates "confusion for employees, investors, and analysts as to who is really leading the business."[34] It also creates resentment among the other directors because their voices are not always heard. In addition, when the chairman grabs too much power, he or she may attempt to supervise the CEO even though he or she has less business acumen and less specific information than the CEO and management team. As a result, the company's power dynamic goes awry when the roles are separated. The CEO and the directors can feel that they are being dominated by the chairman.

In contrast, a lead director is first and foremost a board member and, separately, a board leader (table 8-2). Although the role is expanding, the lead director remains a facilitator, a representative, and a consensus maker. The lead director is always in frequent discussion and consultation with the other directors; therefore, every director is involved. In addition, the lead director unifies the board; therefore, the lead director, as well as the full board, acts as a counterweight to the power and influence of the CEO. The CEO is not able to divide and conquer in order to push his or her ideas through the board, and the directors are more willing to speak up and put an end to actions that they don't like. On the other hand, the separate chairman may become the sole counterweight to the CEO and leave the board out of a true governing role.

At this point in time, the lead director is able to perform the same duties as a separate chairman without creating troublesome power dynamics in the boardroom. Because of the way the role has developed, the lead director has rarely been an authoritative figure, but rather a facilitator and a liaison to management. As a result, it is unnecessary to separate the roles of the CEO and chairman, and extremely worthwhile to elect a lead director.

TABLE 8-2

**Advantages of the lead director role**

Provides the board with independent leadership

Unifies the board: serves as an effective counterweight to the CEO

Leads the independent directors without creating a second power center on the board

Is able to perform the same duties as a separate chairman

# Notes

1. James C. Worthy and Robert P. Neuschel, *Emerging Issues in Corporate Governance* (Evanston, IL: Northwestern University, J. L. Kellogg School of Management, 1984), 1.

2. Ibid.

3. Ibid.

4. Jay W. Lorsch and Elizabeth McIver, *Pawns or Potentates: The Reality of America's Corporate Boards* (Boston: Harvard Business School Press, 1989), 96.

5. Courtney C. Brown, *Putting the Corporate Board to Work* (New York: Macmillan, 1976), 118.

6. Ray Garrett, "Corporate Directors and the Federal Securities Laws," (address to the 13th annual Corporate Counsel Institute, Northwestern University School of Law, Chicago, IL, October 3, 1974).

7. Lorsch and MacIver, *Pawns or Potentates*, 17.

8. Stratford P. Sherman, "Pushing Corporate Boards to Be Better," *Fortune*, July 18, 1988.

9. Nell Minow and Robert Monks, *Watching the Watchers* (Cambridge, MA: Blackwell, 1996), 291.

10. Lorsch and MacIver, *Pawns or Potentates*, 184.

11. Ibid.

12. Martin Lipton and Jay W. Lorsch, "A Modest Proposal for Improved Corporate Governance," *The Business Lawyer*, November 1992.

13. Jay Lorsch, interview by author, February 18, 2011.

14. Nell Minow and Robert A. G. Monks, *Corporate Governance,* 4th ed. (West Sussex, England: John Wiley & Sons, 2008).

15. Ira Millstein is a senior partner at Weil, Gotshal & Manges LLP and the Senior Associate Dean for Corporate Governance and the Eugene F. Williams Jr. Visiting Professor in Competitive Enterprise and Strategy at the Yale School of Management.

16. Judith H. Dobrzynski, "Chairman to Step Down in G.M. Shift," *The New York Times*, December 5, 1995.

17. Joseph Penbera, "What Lead Directors Do," *MIT Sloan Management Review* 50, no. 4 (Summer 2009).

18. Lipton and Lorsch, "A Modest Proposal."

19. National Association of Corporate Directors, *The Report of the NACD Blue Ribbon Commission on Board Leadership* (Washington, DC: Author, 2004).

20. The California Public Employees' Retirement System, *Global Principles of Accountable Corporate Governance* (Sacramento, CA: Author, 2010).

21. RiskMetrics Group, *U.S. Proxy Voting Guidelines Concise Summary* (New York: Author, January 2010).

22. Jeffrey Stein and Bill Baxley, "Drafting Disclosure Relating to Board Leadership and Risk Oversight," The Harvard Law School Forum on Corporate Governance and Financial Regulation, January 3, 2010.

23. Dodd-Frank Wall Street Reform and Consumer Protection Act, Public Law 111-203, July 21, 2010, 54, http://www.gpo.gov/fdsys/pkg/PLAW-111publ203/pdf/PLAW-111publ203.pdf.

24. Spencer Stuart, 2010 Spencer Stuart Board Index, 25th ed., http://content.spencerstuart.com/sswebsite/pdf/lib/SSBI2010.pdf.

25. Tapestry Networks, "The Role and Value of the Lead Director," Lead Director Network ViewPoints, July 30, 2008.

26. 2010 Spencer Stuart Board Index.

27. Tapestry Networks, "The Role and Value of the Lead Director."

28. PricewaterhouseCoopers, Lead Directors: A Study of their Growing Influence and Importance, April 2010, http://www.pwc.com/en_US/us/forensic-services/assets/lead-director-survey.pdf.

29. Tapestry Networks, "The Lead Director's Role in Major Transactions," Lead Director Network ViewPoints, March 29, 2010.

30. Ibid.

31. Ibid.

32. Tapestry Networks, "Enhancing Board Performance," Lead Director Network ViewPoints, December 1, 2010.

33. Tapestry Networks, "The Lead Director's Role in Board Succession Planning," Lead Director Network ViewPoints, March 29, 2010.

34. Tapestry Networks, "Responding to the Changing Regulatory and Legislative Environments," Lead Director Network ViewPoints, March 25, 2009.

# Index

*Note:* Page numbers followed by *f* refer to figures; page numbers followed by *t* refer to tables.

"agency" theory of shareholder value, 11, 85–86, 87

AIG, 144

Albertson's, 65

Andrews, Ken, 56–57, 58

annual strategy retreats, 43, 49–50

Apple Computer, 65

audit committees
  compliance requirements and, 45
  independent directors on, 99
  risk management and, 30, 31
  Sarbanes-Oxley Act requirements and, 13
  strategic engagement and, 52

Bank of America, 150

Bebchuk, Lucian, 84

Beers, Charlotte, 71

Berle, Adolph, 85

bias, and shared information, 123

Black & Decker, 70

Blankfein, Lloyd, 104

Blue Ribbon Commission on Board Leadership, NACD, 134, 139, 160–161

board books
  independent directors and, 99–100
  strategy information in, 43, 50–51

board chairs
  boardroom dynamics and, 44

public disclosure of structure for, 133, 162–163
  separate chairman and CEO model, 133–135, 142, 144, 151–154, 158, 159, 161, 163, 170–171
  *See also* board governance; independent chairs; nonexecutive board chairs

board committees
  communication from, 116
  group dynamics and, 116
  strategic engagement and, 51
  time allotted to work of, 42–43
  *See also* audit committees; compensation committees; governance committees; nominating and governance committees; risk-management committees

board governance, 97–112
  agreement on group's role in, 119
  basic guidelines for, 112
  board chair who is not a CEO and, 109–111
  CEO control of boards and, 135–136
  CEO without a nonexecutive chair and, 105–107
  combined board chair and CEO roles and, 107–109, 125, 136, 137*f*, 139, 139*t*–141*t*, 170–171

board governance (*continued*)
  composition and size of boards
    and, 115
  executive sessions without the CEO
    present, 101–102, 107–108, 138
  experience of board chairs and,
    109–110
  external proposals for changes to,
    98, 159–162
  governance experts and, 98, 105
  imperial CEO model and, 135–136
  impact of financial crises on, 3
  importance of role perspectives in,
    97–98, 112
  independent chairs and, 147
  independent directors and, 98–105,
    107
  interview study of directors on, 10
  legislative reforms in, 98, 136,
    141, 159
  management role separated from,
    105, 107, 108
  Medtronic examples of, 105–107,
    108, 110–111
  negative group dynamics and, 114
  position on board and perspectives
    on, 97–98
  power balance between CEOs and
    independent directors and, 98
  public disclosure of structure for,
    133, 162–163
  responsibility for management of
    board and, 124–125
  separate chairman and CEO model
    and, 133–135, 142, 144, 151–154,
    158, 159, 161, 163, 170–171
  stock exchange listing
    requirements and, 159, 160t
board meetings
  board leadership roles and, 139t
  board's understanding of company
    and frequency of, 18

communication from CEOs
    between, 100
  executive session and updates from
    CEOs at beginning of, 100
  executive sessions without the
    CEO present at, 101–102,
    107–108, 138
  focus on strategy in agendas for,
    42–43, 51–52
  independent directors and, 99
board members. *See* directors
boards of directors
  board member behavior and, 115
  board process best practices and,
    115–116
  CEO evaluation by, 51–52
  check-the-box mentality and, 10, 98
  clarity about role of, 34–35, 34f,
    41–42, 116
  committee work on, 42–43
  complexity of companies and
    information available to, 8–9
  compliance and, 14–15, 34, 34f, 42
  composition and size of, 115
  decision-making responsibility of, 22
  degree of confidence in CEO held
    by, 22–23
  dynamics of. *See* group dynamics
  effectiveness of, 34–35, 34f
  election of directors to, 33
  emphasis on independent directors
    on, 125
  evaluation of work of, 52, 116,
    168–169
  executive compensation and, 42,
    51, 80, 81
  financial skills of, 18–19
  focus on the human element in, 2
  future of, 2–3
  impact of financial crises on, 3
  interview study of directors on
    role of, 11, 13–16

leadership of, 115–116

majority-voting rules on, 33

management's relationship with, 12, 14, 15–16, 22–25, 34–35, 34f

members of. *See* directors

negative group dynamics on, 113–141

performance monitoring by, 42, 44, 48–49, 49f

relationship between shareholders and, 32, 33

reliance on information from CEOs and, 19–20

resource allocation decisions by, 49, 52

responsibility for management of, 124–125

risk management and, 15, 29–32, 34, 34f, 42

shareholder activism and, 42

strategy and oversight by, 15, 19, 26–28, 34, 34f, 37–52

succession planning and, 12, 28–29, 34, 34f, 41–42, 53–74

time spent on strategy by, 37–38, 44, 45, 52

transition to new CEO and, 72–73

understanding of company by, 11, 17–21, 34–35, 34f, 38

understanding of industry by, 38, 43, 44–45

bonuses, 85, 86, 103, 109

Booz Allen Hamilton, 55, 65, 71

Bower, Joseph L., 2, 53–74

Breen, Ed, 150

Buffett, Warren, 84

Bush, George W., 104

*Business Lawyer, The* (journal), 157

business model, board's understanding of, 17

Business Roundtable, 86

California Public Employee Retirement System (CalPERS), 161–162

CEOs

board governance and, 98

boards controlled by, 135–136

board's evaluation of, 51–52

board's reliance on information from, 19–20

circularity problem in, 136, 137f

combined board chair and CEO roles, 107–109, 125, 136, 137f, 170–171

communication between board meetings from, 100

compensation of. *See* executive compensation

degree of confidence in, 22–23

description of job of, 56–59

as directors on outside boards, 112

disabled CEO and transition in leadership, 143

executive session and updates from, at beginning of board meetings, 100

financial performance and, 54, 55, 56t, 57, 59

imperial CEO model of boards, 135–136

independent chairs and, 138, 147, 148

independent directors and, 98, 100

integration of the specialist functions by, 57

lead directors and, 25, 163–164, 170

nonexecutive board chairs and, 105–107

public disclosure of structure for, 133, 162–163

relationship between boards and, 22–23, 24

resignation of, 103, 106, 168

CEOs (*continued*)
 resource allocation decisions by, 57
 responsibility for current
  operations and, 58
 risk management and, 31
 role of boards in oversight of, 15
 separate chairman and CEO
  model, 133–135, 142, 144,
  151–154, 158, 159, 161, 163,
  170–171
 shareholder communications
  and, 33
 strategy and, 41, 42, 58–59
 succession planning and role of,
  28–29, 53–54, 60, 63, 70–73
 tasks performed by, 56–57
 turnover rates for, 55, 83
 understanding of company by, 17,
  18, 19–20
CFOs
 median total compensation for, 79*f*
 shareholder communications
  and, 33
 stock buybacks and, 100
chairs. *See* board chairs; board
  governance
chief executive officers. *See* CEOs
chief financial officers. *See* CFOs
Chrysler, 71
circularity problem in combined board
  chair and CEO roles, 136, 137*f*
Citigroup, 40, 58
coaching, 67, 138
coalition formation, 122, 128–129
codetermination movement, 131
Cohn, Gary, 104
collaboration
 executive compensation related
  to, 83
 independent chairs and, 148–149
collectivist feeling, in boardroom
  group dynamics, 119, 129

committees. *See* board committees
  and other named committees
communication
 board committees and, 116
 board leadership roles and, 140*t*
 from CEOs between board
  meetings, 100, 107
 independent chairs and, 142
 lead directors and, 167
 between management and boards,
  19–21, 34–35, 34*f*
 between shareholders and boards,
  33, 167
Compaq, 39
compensation. *See* executive
  compensation
compensation committees
 candidates in succession planning
  and, 70
 compliance requirements
  and, 45
 independence of, 80
 lump-sum payments and, 85
 negotiations and, 81, 83, 84–85, 93
 surveys on executive compensation
  and, 84
Compensation Discussion and
  Analysis (CD&A), 10-K reports,
  84, 86, 89
competitive advantage, strategy for
  sustaining, 47–48
competitors
 board's understanding of, 17
 strategic engagement and
  understanding of, 46, 51
complex companies
 adequacy of information given to
  board in, 8–9, 17
 challenges to boards from, 8–9
 definition of, 8
 interview study of directors on
  boards of, 9–35, 10*t*

compliance, and role of boards, 14–15, 34, 34f, 42

*Concept of Corporate Strategy, The* (Andrews), 56–57

conflict
between CEOs and independent chairs, 144
group dynamics and, 121–122

conformity, and group dynamics, 117–119, 121, 127

Congress
board leadership guidelines from, 162
tax code on executive compensation and, 89

consultants, and executive compensation, 81–82, 84, 86, 87

corporate boards. *See* boards

Corporate Governance Initiative, Harvard Business School, 8

credibility of independent chairs, 146

crisis management, and lead directors, 25, 168

culture of company
lead director selection and, 170
new CEO's understanding of, 65
outsider candidates and, 70–71

customer focus
continuity in CEO leadership and, 55
strategy and, 45–46, 51

customer value propositions, and strategy, 46–47, 48

Daimler, 71

decision-making responsibility
boardroom group dynamics and, 121, 127
excessive conformity and, 121
lead directors and, 169
relationship between boards and management and, 22

succession planning and, 29

Delaware, statutes on directors in, 13–14

Delaware Court of Chancery, 86

directors
board books for, 43, 50–51
board leadership and, 115–116
board's role in strategy and experience of, 27–28
candidates in succession planning and, 69–70
clarity about board's role and, 34–35, 34f, 41–42, 116
communication between board meetings for, 100
dynamics among. *See* group dynamics
election of, 33, 80
executive compensation issues and, 78–79, 85, 86
external proposals for changes to, 156–157, 158–159
feedback on performance of, 136, 137f, 138
financial skills of, 18–19
independence of. *See* independent directors
independent chairs and, 137–138
interview study of, 9–35, 10t
quality and experience of, 12–13
reliance on information from CEOs and, 19–20
Sarbanes-Oxley Act requirements and, 13, 15
shareholders' complaints about executive compensation and, 32–33
strategic information briefs for, 49, 50–51
strategy engagement by, 37–52
time spent on strategy by, 37–38, 44, 45, 52

directors (*continued*)
   understanding of company by, 11,
     17–21, 34–35, 34*f*, 38, 44
   understanding of industry by, 38,
     43, 44–45
Disney, 152
dissent, and group dynamics,
   117–118, 127
diversity, and group dynamics,
   119–120, 125
Dodd-Frank bill (later Dodd–Frank
   Wall Street Reform and
   Consumer Protection Act), 8, 33,
   42, 133, 162–163
DuPont, 150

economic crises. *See* financial crises
election of directors, 33, 80, 108
Enron, 7, 18, 89, 98, 114, 158
enterprise risk management
   (ERM), 31
evaluation
   of boards of directors, 52, 116,
     168–169
   development of talent in
     succession planning and, 67
   lead directors and, 168–169
executive compensation, 77–94
   "agency" theory of shareholder
     value and, 85–86, 87
   amount of pay in, 78–79
   background to current policies in,
     81–88
   bonuses and, 85, 86, 103, 109
   causes and consequences of
     escalation of, 88–89
   CEO turnover rate and, 83
   collaborative effort of senior
     executives tied to, 83
   comparison across countries for,
     78, 78*f*

   components of, 86–87, 87*t*
   consultants and, 81–82, 84
   development of talent in
     succession planning and, 67
   economic outcomes of company
     and, 92–94
   elevator effect on pay in, 85
   financial crises and concerns about,
     77, 88, 92
   golden parachutes and, 84–85, 87,
     87*t*, 93
   incentive pay schemes and, 78
   income distribution statistics and,
     78, 80*f*
   larger societal questions and,
     80–81, 89–92
   lump-sum payments in, 84–85, 87*t*,
     88, 93
   make-whole payments in, 84, 85,
     87, 87*t*, 93
   market fallacy in, 83–85
   median total compensation for
     CEOs and subordinates, 78–79, 79*f*
   motivational model in, 82, 88
   need to revise paradigm of, 89–92
   negotiations on, 81, 83, 84–85
   performance of company linked
     to, 78–79, 84, 86, 87*t*, 88, 93
   public concerns about, 77–78
   range of solutions for problems in,
     79–81
   ratio of average CEO pay to
     average worker pay, 78–79, 79*t*
   role of boards in, 42, 51, 81
   SEC Form 10-K reports on, 7–8, 84
   shareholders' complaints about,
     32–33, 85
   shareholder voice ("say on pay")
     on, 8, 33, 89
   stock price of firm and, 80, 85–86,
     88, 92

surveys on, 84, 88
taxation of, 89
executive sessions of board meetings
   board leadership roles and, 140t
   with CEO for updates, 100
   lead directors and, 164
   without CEO present, 101–102,
      107–108, 138
experience of directors, 12–13

facilitation, and lead directors, 108,
   140t, 164, 167, 169, 171
feedback
   CEO's performance and, 106, 109,
      164–165
   chair's performance and, 109, 149
   combined CEO and chair roles
      and, 140t
   director's performance and, 69,
      116, 127, 136, 137f, 138
   manager's performance and, 67
   motivation from, 93
financial crises
   CEO performance and, 57
   concerns about executive
      compensation and, 77, 88, 92
   differences between problems
      encountered in 2008/2009 and in
      2002, 8
   impact on corporate governance
      and boards of, 8
   interview study of directors on,
      9–35, 10t
   lead directors and, 162–163
   leadership during, 104
   legislative and regulatory changes
      after, 7–8
   responsibilities of boards and,
      7, 14
   risk management and, 29–30,
      31–32

financial performance, and CEOs, 54,
   55, 56t, 57, 59
financial services firms
   board leadership changes and,
      162–163
   board's oversight of, 8, 27
   understanding of company by
      board of, 17–18
financial statements, 52
Fiorina, Carly, 39
five-year strategic plans, 43
Form 10-K reports, 7–8, 30, 84
Friedman, Jessie, 84

Galli, Joseph, 70
Garrett, Ray, 157
General Electric (GE)
   Immelt at, 66, 67–69
   succession planning at, 60, 66,
      67–69
   Welch at, 60, 66, 68, 69, 85
General Instruments, 150
General Motors (GM), 40, 144, 158
George, William, 2, 97–112
Gerstner, Lou, 71
Gilmartin, Raymond, 2, 155–171
Glass Lewis, 10
globalization
   CEO leadership and, 55, 59
   directors' understanding of
      industry and, 44
   future of boards and, 3
   resource allocation by CEOs
      and, 57
Global Principles of Accountable
   Corporate Governance (CalPERS),
   161–162
golden parachutes, 84–85, 87,
   87t, 93
Goldman Sachs, 104–105
governance. See board governance

governance committees
  management's relationship with, 25
  *See also* nominating and
    governance committees
Greenbury, Sir Richard, 59
group dynamics, 113–141
  board committees and, 116
  board member behavior and, 115
  board process best practices and,
    115–116
  coalition formation and, 122,
    128–129
  degree of dissent and, 117–118, 127
  diversity of thought and, 119–120
  collectivist feeling and, 119, 129
  directors' participation and, 44
  effective board leadership and
    processes and, 114, 115–116
  Enron example of failures in, 114
  excessive conformity and, 121
  framing questions and, 127–128
  group polarization and, 124
  groupthink and, 121
  habitual routines and, 122–123
  independent chairs and, 144–145
  individual board member's role in,
    126–129
  leader's role and, 120
  managing tensions in, 124–126
  minority viewpoints and, 117–118,
    127
  negative group conflict and,
    121–122
  pathologies in, 121–124
  pluralistic ignorance and, 123
  power tactics and politicking
    and, 122
  psychological safety and, 118–119
  shared information bias and, 123
  social cohesion and, 117
  social loafing and, 123–124
  tensions and trade-offs in, 116–117

group polarization, 124
groupthink, 24, 117, 118, 119, 121,
  125, 127

habitual routines, 122–123
Harvard Business School
  CEO compensation paradigm
    and, 91
  Corporate Governance Initiative
    of, 8
  executive programs at, 60
  focus on the human element in the
    boardroom at, 2
Hewlett-Packard Company (HP),
  38–41
Hurd, Mark, 39–40

IBM, 39, 58, 65, 66, 71
Immelt, Jeff, 66, 67–69
incentive plans
  comparison across countries for,
    78, 78f
  compensation plans with, 86, 87t
  consultants on, 81–82
  dysfunctional behavior promoted
    by, 79
  economic outcomes of company
    and, 92–94
  longer-term performance of
    company linked to, 93
  motivational model in, 82, 88
  public concerns about, 78
independent chairs, 133–154
  absence of CEOs and, 138
  advantages of, 142–143
  board leadership by, 115–116, 149
  board member as counterbalance
    to, 149
  boardroom group dynamics and,
    144–145
  business acumen of, 145–146
  CEO compatibility and, 147

CEO effectiveness and, 143–144
CEO relationship with, 148
CEOs after retirement as, 141–142
characteristics of right person in,
    145–148, 145t
characteristics of right process in,
    145t, 148–149
clarity about role of, 148
collaboration by, 148–149
conflicts between CEOs and, 144
credibility of, 146
directors and, 137–138
durability of role of, 143
interpersonal skills of, 146
lead director as, 150–152
leadership skills of, 146–147
motivation of, 147
NACD commission on, 134,
    160–161
need for, 135–136
oversight of board's processes by,
    124–125, 137
potential issues for, 143–145
preconditions for effectiveness of,
    145, 145t
public pressure for, 133
reasons for implementing, 137–139
recommendation on
    implementing, 152–154
selection of, 149
separation of CEO roles from,
    133–135
independent directors
  as advocates for strong board
    governance, 99, 101–102
  balance of power between CEOs
    and, 98
  board books for, 99–100
  board governance and, 97, 98–105,
    107
  CEOs on outside boards as, 112
  challenges for, 98–99

election of lead directors and, 108
emphasis on, 125
executive compensation and, 79–80
increase in number of, 12
independent chairs and, 149
industry knowledge of, 19, 38, 43,
    44–45, 99
information updates provided to,
    99–100
lead directors and, 24, 44, 115,
    164–165
leadership roles in crises and, 99,
    103–105
leadership succession and, 99,
    102–103
principal areas of contribution
    by, 99
regulatory emphasis on, 12–13, 19
shareholders and, 167
sound advice and probing
    questions from, 99–101
strategic engagement of, 37
industry knowledge
  board composition and size
    and, 115
  directors and, 38, 43, 44–45, 99
  independent chairs and, 145–146
  new CEOs and, 65
  outsider candidates and, 70, 71
information on companies
  board books for, 43, 50–51
  broader sources for, 21
  challenges to boards and need
    for, 23
  complex companies and adequacy
    of, 8–9, 17
  diversity of thought and sharing
    of, 120
  independent directors and need for
    updates on, 99–100, 107
  lead directors and, 163, 165, 169
  need to "dig deeper" for, 20–21

information on companies (*continued*)
   reliance on CEOs for, 19–20
   shared bias regarding, 123
   strategic information brief for
      updates on, 49, 50–51
   strategy and lack of, 43
   understanding of company by
      board and, 11, 17–21
"inside-outsider" candidates in
   succession planning, 65–66,
   69–70, 72, 73
insider candidates in succession
   planning, 28, 54, 55, 56t, 59–64,
   66–70, 71, 102
institutional investors
   demand for governance changes
      from, 159–160, 161, 162
   executive compensation and, 78
   future of boards and, 2
Intel, 65
interpersonal skills of independent
   chairs, 146
interview study of directors of
   complex companies, 9–35
   companies by industry and size in,
      9, 10t
   definition of complex company in, 8
   description of prerecession boards
      by, 12–13
   effectiveness of boards viewed by,
      34–35, 34f
   government regulations and rules
      viewed by, 9–10
   long-term perspective of directors
      in, 11
   management succession and
      development and, 28–29
   relationship with management
      viewed by, 22–25
   responsibility for successful
      governance by board viewed
      by, 10

   risk management and, 29–32
   role of boards in, 13–16
   selection of interviewees for, 9
   shareholder organizations viewed
      by, 10–11
   six areas analyzed in, 11–32
   strategy oversight by, 26–28
   topics not covered in, 32–33
   understanding of company viewed
      by, 17–21
investor relations executives, 33
IRS, 96

Jensen, Michael, 11, 85
Johnson, Larry, 65

Kallasvuo, Olli-Pekka, 59
keiretsu, 131
Khurana, Rakesh, 41, 64, 77–94
Kozlowski, Dennis, 150
Krol, Jack, 150

Lafley, A. G., 66
laws and legislation
   board governance and, 98, 136,
      141, 159
   financial crises and passage of, 7–8
   future of boards and, 2–3
   role of boards and, 13–14
lawyers and legal staff
   executive compensation and, 86
   role of boards in compliance and,
      14–15
   shareholder proposals and, 33
Lead Director Network, 166, 168
lead directors, 155–171
   adoption of, 159, 161f
   advantages of, 150, 156, 171t
   board chair and, 155–156
   board development and, 168–169
   board leadership by, 115–116, 139,
      139t–141t, 150–152

boardroom dynamics and, 44
CalPERS on, 161–162
CEO evaluations and succession
    and, 167
combined board chair and CEO
    roles and, 108
crisis management and, 25, 168
directors in interview study on,
    24–25
disadvantages of, 150–151
durability of role of, 143
expanding role of, 165–166
facilitator role of, 108, 140t, 164,
    167, 169, 171
financial crisis and, 162–163
independent directors and election
    of, 108
independent directors as, 24,
    44, 115
initial concept of roles of, 157–158
leadership by, 157–158, 171
management and, 24–25, 158, 160,
    164, 167–168, 171
NACD commission on, 160–161
need for independent board
    leadership and, 156–157
negotiations in major transactions
    and, 167–168
nonexecutive board chairs and,
    107, 151, 170–171
oversight of board's processes
    by, 125
possible explanations for lack of
    adoption of, 151–152
relationship between management
    and, 24–25
role and responsibilities of, 163–165
rotation of position of, 166
selection of, 169–170
shareholder communication
    and, 167
strong-leader tension and, 120

succession planning and, 167, 170
leadership
    boardroom group dynamics and,
        114, 115–116, 120, 122
    disabled CEO and transition in, 143
    external proposals for changes to,
        156–157, 159–160, 162
    independent chairs and, 146–147
    independent directors and, 99,
        103–105
    insider candidates and
        development of, 56, 72
    lead directors and, 157–158, 171
    need for independence in, 135–136
    negative conflict and, 122
    outsider candidates in succession
        and, 70, 71
    public disclosure of structure for,
        133, 162–163
    separation of chair and CEO roles
        in, 133–135
leadership succession. See succession
    planning
Lipton, Marty, 150, 157–158, 159
Lorsch, Jay M., 2, 7–35, 53, 77–94,
    134, 150, 157–158, 159
lump-sum payments, 84–85, 87t, 88, 93

McDonald's, 28
McKinsey & Company, 82
McKinsey Quarterly, 37–38
McNerney, James, 65
majority-voting rules, 33
make-whole payments, 84, 85, 87,
    87t, 93
management
    board chair roles and, 105, 107, 108
    board leadership and, 115
    board's role and, 116
    complex companies and
        information flow to boards
        from, 8–9

management (*continued*)
  decision-making responsibility of, 22
  information on strategy from, 50, 51
  lead directors and, 24–25, 158, 160,
    164, 167–168, 171
  questions on strategy and, 45–48
  relationship between boards and,
    12, 22–25, 34–35, 34f
  reliance of boards for information
    from, 19–21
  requests for information from,
    23–24
  role of boards in, 14, 15–16
  strategy definition by, 26, 42
  succession process and work of, 67,
    71–72
management succession. *See*
  succession planning
managers
  acceptance of lead directors by, 160
  need to revise paradigm of
    business and, 91
Marks & Spencer, 59, 63
Means, Gardiner, 85
Meckling, William, 85
Medtronic, 105–107, 108, 110–111
meetings. *See* board meetings
members of boards. *See* directors
mentoring, 67, 69, 73
Merchant, Kenneth, 2, 113–141
Microsoft, 65
Millstein, Ira, 158
Millstein Center for Corporate
  Governance and Performance,
  Yale University, 133
minority viewpoints, 117–118, 127
monthly progress reports from
  CEOs, 100
motivation
  executive compensation as, 82, 88
  individual chairs and, 147
Motorola, 150

Nadler, David A., 133–154
NASDAQ, 159
National Association of Corporate
  Directors (NACD), 134, 139,
  160–161
Newell, 70
New York Stock Exchange (NYSE),
  107, 159, 167
Nokia, 59
nominating and governance
  committees
  evaluation of board against
    strategy by, 52
  lead directors and, 167
  nonexecutive chair selection and,
    153
  transition to new CEO and, 72–73
nonexecutive board chairs
  advantages of, 142–143
  board governance structure and,
    153
  CEOs and board governance and,
    105–107
  description of role of, 141–142
  development of talent for, 153
  independence of. *See* independent
    chairs
  lead directors and, 107, 151,
    170–171
  leadership role of, 139, 139t–141t
  potential issues for, 143–145
  recommendation for use of, 152,
    153–154
  selection of, 152–153

Ogilvy & Mather, 71
Oliver Wyman, 135
options, in executive compensation,
  81, 86, 87t
outsider candidates in succession
  planning, 55, 56t, 59, 61, 62,
  64–65, 70–71, 93, 102

Palepu, Krishna, 2, 37–52

Palmisano, Sam, 58, 66

Paton, Arch, 82

Paulson, Henry, 104

PepsiCo, 65

performance of firms

board's role in monitoring, 42, 44, 49

bonuses tied to, 86

executive compensation linked to, 78–79, 82, 84, 86, 87t, 88, 93

incentive plans and, 93

monitoring strategy versu monitoring of, 48–49, 49f

motivational model in executive compensation and, 82, 88

succession planning and, 65

performance of candidates, and succession planning, 62–63, 64f, 65, 67, 69

performance of directors, evaluation of, 136

Pick, Katharina, 2, 113–141

pluralistic ignorance, 123

polarization, in group dynamics, 124

politicking, 122

power tactics, 122

presiding directors

advantages of, 156

crises and role of, 25

initial concept of, 157, 166

number of companies using title, 166

See also lead directors

PricewaterhouseCoopers, 166

Prince, Charles, 58

Procter & Gamble, 65, 66, 158

profitability, and strategic engagement, 46–47

progress reports from CEOs, 100

proxy advisory firms, 11, 159, 162

proxy statements, 33

psychological safety, 118–119

public opinion

executive compensation in, 78

independent chairs and, 133

quarterly earnings announcements, 42

recruitment, and succession planning, 62, 63, 67, 68, 69

regulation

financial crises and tightening of, 7–8

future of boards and, 2–3

independence of directors and, 13, 19, 44

role of boards and, 13

shareholder influence over companies and, 33

Regulation FD (Fair Disclosure), SEC, 167

*Report of the Blue Ribbon Commission on Board Leadership* (NACD), 134, 139, 160–161

resignation of CEOs, 103, 106, 168

resource allocation decisions

CEOs and, 57

strategy and, 49, 52

retention bonuses, 85

retreats, annual strategy, 43, 49–50

risk management

audit committees and, 30, 31

board's understanding of, 18, 32

CEOs and, 31

disagreements over responsibility for, 29–30

role of boards in, 12, 15, 29–32, 34, 34f, 42

risk-management committees, 30

RiskMetrics Group, 10, 162

Rose, Stuart, 63

Salsbury, Peter, 63

SAP, 57

Sarbanes-Oxley Act (SOX), 7, 13, 15,
26, 31, 42, 107, 136, 141, 159
"say on pay" approach to executive
compensation, 8, 33, 89
Schremp, Juergen, 71
scientific management, 82
Sculley, John, 65
search firms, 64–65, 103
Sears, 40
Securities and Exchange Commission
(SEC), 7–8, 30, 84, 167
senior executives
compensation of. *See* executive
compensation
executive compensation paradigm
held by, 81
market for, 83–84
succession process and work of, 67,
71–72
*See also* CEOs
shared information bias, 123
shareholder activism, 42, 115, 162
shareholder organizations, 10–11
shareholder proposals, 98
shareholders
access to proxy statements by, 33
complaints about executive
compensation from, 32–33, 77,
78, 79, 85
corporation as a social institution
and, 90
election of directors and, 80
information for boards from, 21
lead directors and communication
with, 167
relationship between boards and,
32, 33, 42
"say on pay" approach to
executive compensation and, 8,
33, 89
*See also* institutional investors

shareholder value
executive compensation tied to
"agency" theory of, 85–86, 87
short-term focus on, 11
size of boards of directors, 115
size of companies, growth in, 3
Smale, John, 158
Smith, Jack, 158
social cohesion, 117
social loafing, 118–119, 123–124
Spencer Stuart, 163
staggered boards, 33
Stempel, Robert, 158
stock, in executive compensation, 81,
86, 87*t*, 88
stock buybacks, 100–101
stock price, and executive
compensation amount, 80,
85–86, 88, 92
strategic information briefs, 49, 50–51
strategic plans, five-year, 43
strategy, 37–52
active participation by boards in,
38, 42
amount of time spent by directors
on, 37–38, 44, 45, 52
annual retreats for, 43, 49–50
board agendas and focus on, 42–43,
51–52
board governance and, 106
CEO's role in, 41, 58–59
clarity about board's role and,
41–42
committee work integrated with, 51
competitive landscape and, 46
critical barriers to board's
engagement in, 41–44
critical board functions and board's
knowledge of, 38
customer need being targeted in,
45–46

dysfunctional boardroom
   dynamics and, 44
framework for engagement in,
   44–52
Hewlett-Packard example of
   neglecting, 38–41
integration of general board work
   with work on, 45
lack of information in, 43
longer-term perspective in, 26–27
management's role in defining, 26
monitoring execution of, 48–52, 49f
new CEOs in succession planning
   and impact on, 71
partnership between board and
   management in, 42
passive review and approval of, 38
profitability and, 46–47
resource allocation decisions and,
   49, 52
role of boards in, 12, 15, 19, 26–28,
   34, 34f, 37
questions for understanding, 45–48
strategic information brief for
   updates on, 49, 50–51
succession planning and
   knowledge of, 41, 52, 61
sustaining competitive advantage
   and, 47–48
understanding of company and,
   19, 38
understanding of industry and, 38,
   43, 44–45
succession planning, 53–74
   age of candidates in, 103
   assignments for insider candidates
      in, 61, 62, 66, 67, 68–69, 72, 102
   bias against insider candidates in,
      60–61, 63
   CEO turnover rate and, 55
   challenges in, 56, 62–63

choice of "charismatic leaders" in,
   41–42
contingency plan ("hit by a bus"
   scenario) and, 102
corporate culture and, 65, 70–71
criteria for, 62, 67
decision-making responsibility in,
   29, 54, 62–66, 70, 72
developing candidates for, 59–61,
   62, 67, 72
difficulties of CEO jobs and, 54–55
executive compensation and, 85
Hewlett-Packard example of
   neglecting strategy and impact
   on, 38–41
identifying pool of candidates in,
   67, 72, 73, 102, 103
Immelt at GE as example of,
   67–69, 68t
incumbent CEO's role in, 53–54,
   63, 70, 71, 72, 73
incumbent to insider transition in,
   66–70
incumbent to outsider transition
   in, 70–71
independent directors and, 99,
   102–103, 104–105
in-house candidates and, 28, 54, 55,
   56t, 59–61, 62, 63–64, 71, 102
"inside-outsider" candidates in,
   65–66, 69–70, 72, 73
job of CEOs and, 56–59
knowledge of strategic needs and,
   41, 52
lead directors and, 167, 170
leadership in times of crisis and,
   104–105
legal responsibility of board in, 53
managing process of, 66–71, 103
mentoring and coaching in, 67,
   69, 73

succession planning (*continued*)
  outsider candidates in, 55, 56*t*, 59,
    61, 62, 64–65, 70–71, 102
  performance and action in,
    62–63, 64*f*
  planning process used in, 60
  reaching consensus in, 70
  reasons for deferring, 29
  recruitment of talent to company
    and, 62, 63, 67, 68, 69
  role of boards in, 12, 28–29, 34, 34*f*,
    41–42, 62–66, 69–74
  search firms and, 64–65, 103
  tenure of insider versus outsider
    CEOs in, 71
  transition to new CEO and, 72–73
  understanding of industry and, 65
surveys on executive compensation,
    84, 88

Target, 109
tax code, and executive
    compensation, 89

Taylor, Frederick, 82
technological change, 3, 17
10-K reports, 7–8, 30, 84
3M, 65
top management. *See* senior
    management
turnover rates for CEOs, 55, 83
Tyco International, 7, 150, 158

U.S. Internal Revenue Service
    (IRS), 86
U.S. Securities and Exchange
    Commission (SEC), 7–8, 30,
    84, 167

Visa International, 130–131

Welch, Jack, 60, 66, 68, 69, 85
Winkelried, Jon, 104
WorldCom, 7, 158
Yale University, Millstein Center for
    Corporate Governance and
    Performance, 133

# About the Contributors

JOSEPH L. BOWER is a Baker Foundation Professor of Business Administration and has been teaching general management at Harvard Business School for more than forty-five years. Among his more than a dozen books is *The CEO Within: Why Inside Outsiders Are the Key to Succession Planning*. He is a director of Anika Therapeutics, Inc., Lowes, New America High Income Fund, and Sonesta International Hotels. He holds a bachelor's, MBA, and DBA from Harvard University.

BILL GEORGE is a Professor of Management Practice at Harvard Business School, where he has taught leadership since 2004. He is the author of several books on leadership, including *Authentic Leadership: Rediscovering the Secrets to Creating Lasting Value*. He is the former Chairman and CEO of Medtronic, which he joined in 1989 and where he also served as President and Chief Operating Officer. He currently serves as a director of ExxonMobil and Goldman Sachs and has also recently served on the boards of Novartis and Target, among others. He holds an MBA degree from Harvard Business School.

RAYMOND V. GILMARTIN is an Adjunct Professor at Harvard Business School. He is the former Chairman, President, and CEO of Merck & Co. Prior to that he had served as Chairman, President, and CEO of Becton Dickinson. He now serves on the boards of General Mills and Microsoft. He received his MBA from Harvard Business School in 1968.

RAKESH KHURANA is the Marvin Bower Professor of Leadership Development at the Harvard Business School. Among his several books is *Searching for a Corporate Savior: The Irrational Quest for*

*Charismatic CEOs.* He serves on the board of American Family Mutual Insurance. Khurana has a PhD in organizational behavior from Harvard University.

JAY W. LORSCH is the Louis Kirstein Professor of Human Relations at the Harvard Business School, where he has taught and researched for more than forty-seven years. He is the author of many articles and books about boards of directors, including the path-breaking *Pawns or Potentates: The Reality of America's Corporate Boards*, with Elizabeth MacIver, and *Back to the Drawing Board: Designing Corporate Boards for a Complex World*, with Colin B. Carter. He teaches courses to MBAs, Harvard Law students, and executives about corporate boards. He received a DBA from Harvard in 1964 and he has served on the boards of a number of public companies, including Brunswick Corp., Benckiser NV, and CA, Inc.

KENNETH MERCHANT holds the Deloitte & Touche Chair of Accountancy at the University of Southern California. Before joining USC, he taught at Harvard Business School from 1978 to 1990. He is the author of ten books, including *Blind Spots, Biases and Other Pathologies in the Boardroom*, with Katharina Pick. He is a certified public accountant and has a PhD from the University of California, Berkeley. He currently serves on the board of Entropic Communications, Inc., as well as Vericimetry Funds. He has served on the board of Diagnostic Products Corporation and Universal Guardian Holdings, Inc.

DAVID NADLER is vice chairman of Marsh & McLennan Companies. He was the founder of Delta Consulting, which consults to top management groups and boards of directors. He is the author of many books, including *Building Better Boards: A Blueprint for Effective Governance*. He has a PhD in psychology from the University of Michigan and an MBA from Harvard Business School.

KRISHNA PALEPU is the Ross Graham Walker Professor of Business Administration and Senior Associate Dean for International

Development at Harvard Business School. He is the coauthor of many books, including *Winning in Emerging Markets: A Road Map for Strategy and Execution*. In his work with boards he has focused on the board's engagement with strategy. He holds a PhD degree in management from the Massachusetts Institute of Technology.

**KATHARINA PICK** is Clinical Assistant Professor of Organizational Behavior at the Peter F. Drucker & Masatoshi Ito Graduate School of Management at Claremont Graduate University. She is the coauthor with Kenneth Merchant of *Blind Spots, Biases, and Other Pathologies in the Boardroom*. She received her PhD in organizational behavior from Harvard University in June 2005.